That We May Be One

Also by Michael Harper:

* *Let My People Grow*
* *Spiritual Warfare*
  Power for the Body of Christ
  Life in the Holy Spirit
  None Can Guess
  You Are My Sons
  A New Way of Living
  As at the Beginning
  This Is the Day
  The Love Affair
  Walk in the Spirit

* Published in America by Bridge Publishing, Inc.

That We May Be One

Michael Harper

author of *Spiritual Warfare*

Bridge Publishing, Inc.
Publishers of:
LOGOS • HAVEN • OPEN SCROLL

That We May Be One
Copyright © 1983 by Michael Harper. First printed in 1983. All rights reserved. No part of this publication may be reproduced or transmitted in any form or by any means, electronic or mechanical, including photocopy, recording, or any information storage and retrieval system, without permission in writing from the publisher. Printed in Great Britain for Hodder and Stoughton Limited, Mill Road, Dunton Green, Sevenoaks, Kent by Richard Clay (The Chaucer Press) Ltd., Bungay, Suffolk. Hodder and Stoughton Editorial Office: 47 Bedford Square, London WC1B 3DP. American Edition published by Bridge Publishing, Inc., South Plainfield, New Jersey 07080 USA. Printed in the United States of America. Library of Congress Catalog Card Number: 84-70052, ISBN 0-88270-567-9. Published by arrangement with Edward England Books.

Contents

1. Our God Reigns, Thank Goodness 1
2. One God, One People 9
3. Fresh Not New Wineskins..................17
4. No Exclusives 25
5. The Two Structures 39
6. Handling Our Differences 53
7. Neither Slave Nor Free 67
8. Tension Points.........................79
9. Water Baptism, Infants or Adults? 89
10. Traditions, Human or Divine? 103
11. Women, Leaders or Led? 119
12. Apostles and Prophets, True or False? 129
13. The Spotless Church 143
14. I'm Staying in! 155
    Acknowledgments......................161

1
Our God Reigns, Thank Goodness

The well-known hymn "Our God Reigns" was chosen recently for an induction service at an Anglican church. Unfortunately there was a misprint in the order of service which the printer overlooked. The hymn came out as "Our God Resigns." It would be difficult to calculate the number of times our God would have been tempted to resign as He looks down from heaven at the shambles which is usually called "the Church." Fortunately for all of us, He has never done so, and His nature is such He never will. Equally fortunate is that fact that He has never and will never resign himself to the mess that He beholds, but instead He works ceaselessly, in spite of the mountains of human stupidity that He has to circumvent, and has found ways of bringing in His Kingdom and renewing His Church in every century. No, our God is not a resigning God, *He is a reigning God*.

I could have called this book "Renewal Without Tears" because the English word "tear" has two quite different meanings. It is the word for what comes from the eyes when we weep; it is also a word for division. To tear something is to divide it, usually in a harmful or

THAT WE MAY BE ONE

destructive way. The Church all through its long and changing history has needed renewal. It will continue to need it until Christ returns. But renewal has always been a painful thing. It does cause tears. It can also cause division in the Church. Instead of healing the wounds in the Body of Christ it can rub salt in them and even cause more splits. But this is not inevitable. It is not necessary; we can and should find ways by which renewal comes as a blessing and a unifying experience for the Body of Christ. I hope that this book will help to prevent further "tearings" and promote the unity of the Body of Christ, which bears many painful scars from the past and still suffers grievously from its divisions.

But tears of joy and grief will always be part of the renewal scene. The Holy Spirit, when He renews the Church, disturbs it. Some of the disturbance may be because of human sinfulness; but when we have stripped away the human elements and got the divine content in focus, we know that the influence of the Spirit is always to disturb our complacency. In that sense there can be no genuine renewal without pain, and, therefore, tears.

During the 1960s and 1970s many people experienced a new work of the Holy Spirit in their lives. There was a quickening of the spiritual tempo. Then during the 1970s a shadow was cast over these hopes by the emergence of tension points. In the early 1980s splits between churches and within churches became much more common. The main issue was about the

Our God Reigns, Thank Goodness

Church. Some began to believe and say that the old denominational churches at best could only expect superficial renewal. If one wanted all that God wanted, one would have to find it in new "house churches," independent fellowships free from denominational shackles. Some went so far as to teach that this was the only obedient course for Christians to follow.

During the 1960s and 1970s the tension was about the *experience* of the Holy Spirit. Is there or is there not a post-baptism or post-conversion experience called "the baptism in the Holy Spirit?" That brought problems to churches all over the world, but by the 1980s Christians had come to live with one another in spite of their differences. The new point of tension is more serious and is bound to affect people more deeply. It is now about *the Church* rather than Christian experience. The new wine is one thing, fresh wineskins are something else. It is much harder to resolve this one—and still remain together in fellowship. I believe it is possible. But we should have no illusions about the difficulties.

God's way of doing things is often strange, and our way often conflicts with His. Does God simply discard the old churches and replace them with new ones whenever He decides to renew the church? Should all churches be "pure" in the sense of only having true Christians as members, or can the church be a mixture of the good and the bad, the spiritual and the carnal, the dedicated and the half-hearted, the free and the formal, the committed and the nominal, the

THAT WE MAY BE ONE

renewed and the unrenewed? I hope to give some answers to these sorts of questions. I believe many are asking them, and they need to be faced up to and not shirked.

Great damage can be done when we adopt the attitude, "I have no need of you." We are simply condemned to repeat the mistakes of the past, and to find the task of Christian unity that much harder. Some have thought it their duty to denounce the historic churches, pouring scorn on their rigidity, only to be instrumental themselves in creating new denominations even more rigid and exclusive than those they have come out of.

Although the new independents are experiencing blessing, they have yet to face the problems of second generation renewal. The historic churches have for hundreds of years learned how to handle it. But independent churches often simply create more independent churches; they fragment still further, their idealism tarnished by their inevitable inability to maintain that ideal.

The starting of new churches *seems* to be the simple answer to spiritual decline in the old churches. But in the *long term* it seldom works.

I am writing this for those who are struggling with these issues and who may not realize that the Bible and the past experience of the Church do give us some answers. I am writing for members of the old churches —Roman Catholics, Orthodox, Anglicans and Protestants who are sometimes under pressure to leave

Our God Reigns, Thank Goodness

their "dead" or "half-hearted" churches and join the new, lively and committed fellowships. I am also writing it for those of you who have joined these new "pure" churches and found that they are not so good after all. They are not God's complete answer. You are beginning to realize that you are missing the more balanced, even if less lively, churches you left.

I am also writing for the convinced members of these new churches with the desire that they will come to recognize what God is doing in the historic churches and understand why we are staying in them. I hope we shall not simply be brushed aside as lukewarm compromisers, but regarded as brothers, however misguided they may think we are.

People have always moved from church to church, and with the greater mobility of people and the fruits of ecumenism beginning to be more universal, a growing number of people change their allegiance from one church to another. There is nothing wrong in that provided we do it for the right reasons. It is usually the right course of action when two people from different churches get married for one of them to leave his or her church and join the one which the marriage partner is committed to, or they may both leave and join a new church altogether. Moving from one part of the country to another may necessitate change—or doctrinal convictions may call for a change of church.

Sometimes parents, especially when the Christian education of their children is at stake, may want to change their church. All this can be perfectly legitimate

THAT WE MAY BE ONE

provided we don't become church gypsies moving around as fashion dictates. That will do us no good. There is in all of us a kind of idealism, in which we have our fantasies about the perfect kind of church we want to belong to. We are doomed to be constantly in a state of disillusionment. There are no perfect churches and we shall always have to take the rough with the smooth, just as others have to accept us with our imperfections.

This book is not dealing with these exceptional situations. It is to show that creating altogether new churches in order to experience the new thing that God may be doing, is not always necessary or right. God has a better way, namely to renew the existing church from within. It takes a good deal longer. It is more painful. It requires a high degree of patience and love. We need to be good at forgiving and being forgiven. But it is usually more fruitful and more lasting than the easier and quicker way of starting all over again. God does not want us to take short cuts.

Much of what I am writing about concerns the so-called house churches or independent charismatic fellowships which have sprung up particularly in Britain and North America during the 1970s and 1980s. I know many of their leaders and recognize their spiritual qualities and the integrity of their lives. I have also visited and spoken to some of these fellowships and know that there is a liveliness and commitment amongst them which is often missing in the older churches. I hope in these pages to point out another

Our God Reigns, Thank Goodness

way forward—not to condemn the new independent churches, but to help both sides of this divide find God's way to unity and usefulness in a world desperately in need of the gospel and a united Church to proclaim it.

2
One God, One People

The story of God's dealings with man shows that His perfect will and purpose is that His people be one. The nation of Israel was divided into twelve tribes. But it was always intended to be one nation. There was much that could be done by individuals within that one nation. But God's people were never permitted to withdraw from that nation and start a new one. U.D.I.s (Unilateral Declaration of Independence) were forbidden. The temptation to do so must have been at times hard to resist. Constantly throughout the pages of the Old Testament God's people rebelled against Him, worshiped idols, went after other gods and committed many acts of spiritual adultery. The rulers of Israel—the judges and the kings—were more often than not corrupt and evil in their ways. The Old Testament presents an honest account of the sinfulness of Israel's rulers and people. There are more bad kings than good ones. The people of God seem more often in a state of spiritual decline and even apostasy than in a right and pleasing relationship to God. But at no time during these periods of spiritual degeneration is a policy advanced for forming a new nation from the remnants

THAT WE MAY BE ONE

of the old. The righteous and the unrighteous belong together in the one nation of Israel, and those who are right with God have to suffer often for the sins of others.

In the story of the journey of God's people through the desert of Sinai under the leadership of Moses, there is a striking example of this biblical principle. In Exodus 32 we are told about the impatience of God's people. Moses had disappeared from sight up the mountain, and they had neither heard from him nor seen him for many days. So the people asked Aaron to make them gods: "as for this Moses," they said, "we do not know what has become of him." Under pressure from the people Aaron gave way and together they committed a gross sin of idolatry when they made a golden calf and began to worship it.

Up on the mountain God and Moses discuss this act of rebellion against the law. The Lord reports to Moses what has been going on in his absence at the foot of the mountain. God calls them a "stiff-necked people" and threatens to wipe them out. Then God says to Moses, "But of you I will make a great nation." What a temptation for Moses! God is offering to deal once and for all with the nation of Israel, to wipe it out and start all over again with Moses. The people deserved it. They had sinned and turned their backs on both God and Moses. Here was a literally heaven-sent opportunity for Moses to become great, the founder of a completely new nation. Here was a short cut to all the problems of leading a half-hearted and mixed company of people into the Land of Promise. Now there could

One God, One People

come into existence a pure and dedicated company of people who could take the Kingdom by storm.

But Moses refused this offer categorically. Moses reminded God of the great promises He had made to Abraham, Isaac and Jacob. Moses kept Him to these promises however sinful and degenerate God's people had become. But Moses went further; he said in effect, "What will the Egyptians say? What will their enemies do when they see God wiping the nation out?" What we do to one another as Christians seldom goes unnoticed by the world around us.

In the text Moses challenged God to repent of this plan of action: "repent of this evil against thy people" (v. 12). And we are told He did: "the Lord repented of the evil which He thought to do unto His people." It was one of a number of occasions in which the intercession of Moses saved the people of God.

Can we not see the importance of this in the light of the modern attitudes of some Christians who have separated themselves from those whom they deem unspiritual? Some have set themselves up as the great new nation, the very thing that Moses firmly resisted to the point of urging God to change His mind. That way has never been God's way. God has never allowed an elitist group to separate itself from the rest of His people even for the purest of motives. Rather it has always been His will that they remain one people—with freedom to testify, gather as a renewal group, suffer and if necessary die for the honor of God's name amidst a majority of stubbornly rebellious people.

THAT WE MAY BE ONE

In the following chapter (Exodus 33), we see a perfect example of a pattern which has worked successfully throughout Bible times and for hundreds of years of church history. Even though they were a "stiff-necked people," God still promised to bring them into the Land. The promise was not given on condition of total obedience or perfect behavior. But God did say that He himself would not be amongst them. They would have to make do with an angel. If He went with them, "they would be consumed."

That was all right so far as the people were concerned, but for Moses and his assistant Joshua and "an unknown number of Israelites," it was not good enough. They just had to have communion with God. So while the people stayed in the camp without experiencing the glory of God, Moses took the tent *outside* the camp and called it "the tent of meeting." If people wanted to meet with God, they had to leave the less spiritual Israelites in the camp and walk out to the tent. There the pillar of cloud, symbol of God's presence, was to be found—but *not* within the camp itself. There we are told "the Lord would speak with Moses" and presumably those others who were with him. But Moses did not stay in the tent. He did not forsake the unspiritual Israelites back in the camp. He left Joshua to lead the renewed Israelites, but went back into the camp to minister to the others.

However bad they were, God never gave up His people. There was always a faithful remnant who stayed amongst the rest. But there was also a place

One God, One People

and an opportunity for the spiritually enlightened to have fellowship and meet with God. Then they would go back to the camp, often invoking hostility and persecution from the rest of God's people. Godly people have never been popular; but that is not a sufficient reason for them to leave the rest of the people of God and form a new, exclusive and separate body. God's people, however different their stages of spiritual development or commitment may be, are always one people.

This story in Exodus 33 is not just an isolated incident, but reveals a general principle that runs like a thread through the whole of the Old Testament. God's remedy for sin in the camp was *never* separation or division. He often punished His people, but He never told the obedient and faithful to separate themselves from the rest. The people of God were divided geographically into tribes; but they were not twelve nations—but *one nation*. When the nation later divided into the Northern Kingdom of Israel and the Southern Kingdom of Judah, this was because of human sin, not divine guidance. It was never God's will that the Kingdom should be divided in this way.

It is interesting to notice that God's people went into Canaan as one people. They could have made it at the first attempt, forty years earlier. But because of faithlessness and disobedience they had to wait many years before the way was clear for them to enter into what the Lord had promised. There were a few, like Caleb and Joshua, who were not guilty of unbelief and therefore, presumably could have moved immediately into the Land of Promise. *But they too had to wait until everyone was ready to move in.*

We shall see later how Christians have grappled with the problem of the mixed Church. The policy in both the Western and Eastern Church has always been to "pitch a tent outside the camp." The most important of these "tents" was the monastic movement, which was rooted in the Church, and which gave an opportunity for those who were more dedicated or committed to work out that commitment in terms of worship and service "outside the camp." But they were still part of the camp, and like the "renewed Israelites" returned to it after they had met with God. This was somewhat changed at the time of the Reformation, to the detriment of the Church as a whole. The Church split into innumerable groups, all aspiring to be "faithful to God." Denominationalism was born. It was a tragic hour for the Church and the world. The kingdom became divided against itself. The result in Europe was the wholesale spread of secularism, the French and Russian Revolutions, the birth of Nazism and the development of theological liberalism, which together destroyed the faith of millions. The consequences of Christian disunity have been disastrous. It all began when the divine principles we have been outlining were rejected in favor of independence. It is not the first time that the quest for freedom has instead led to slavery.

When we turn to look at the ministry of the prophets

One God, One People

in the Old Testament, we find exactly the same principle. It is true that some of the prophets tended to be rather aloof from the people. Some of them had "schools" or disciples and lived some distance from the main cities or towns. But they never cut themselves off from the people of God. They were still "one of them." Ezekiel was "among the exiles by the river Chebar" when he received his revelations (Ezek. 1:1). Later we are told that he was sitting in his house "with the elders of Judah sitting before me" when the hand of God came upon him (8:1).

Later the elders sought him out (20:1). The prophets were not escapists. They did not live in ivory towers. They prophesied from amongst the people. Isaiah had his famous vision of God in the Temple itself, although temple worship must have been very formal and in a state of spiritual decline. Jeremiah with great courage and perseverance prophesied the fall of Jerusalem in an eyeball to eyeball confrontation with the kings and national leaders. It was eventually to cost him his life. The prophets never called on the spiritual remnant in Israel to separate itself from the apostate and corrupt. They were to live out their calling in the midst of considerable tension and difficulties.

We have another excellent example of this principle in the work of the last of this long line of prophets whom Jesus himself called "the greatest." John the Baptist fearlessly brought the message of God's word to God's people. But he did not do it in Jerusalem. He did it in the desert. People had to travel out from the

THAT WE MAY BE ONE

towns and cities to hear him. It was as if that tent of meeting had again been placed "outside the camp." Jesus himself went out to meet John the Baptist and to be baptized by him in the river Jordan. But John always sent those who responded to his message, apart from his small band of disciples, back to their towns and cities, and to the synagogues they attended on the sabbath. He did not start a new denomination for his followers. He did not separate himself from the rest of the people of God. He was to die, if you like, a victim of the system—just as his cousin Jesus was to do a short time afterwards. Both John the Baptist and Jesus challenged the system. They both confronted the establishment. But they did so as part of the system, not as a new elitist band of exclusives.

I believe one can go further and say that those who are part of the system have most right to speak out against it. The Old Testament closes with the call of John the Baptist to repent, but not to secede from the one nation of God's people. Did Jesus come to change all that? For the answer to that question we shall have to look closely at what He taught and how His disciples interpreted His teaching.

3

Fresh Not New Wineskins

And no one puts new wine into old wineskins; if he does, the new wine will burst the skins and it will be spilled, and the skins will be destroyed. But new wine must be put into fresh wineskins. and no one after drinking old wine desires new; for he says, "The old is good." (Luke 5:37-39)

Many of us will have heard the argument that goes something like this: "God is pouring out His Spirit. He is giving us new wine. But the old historic churches cannot contain this new wine. So we must start new churches which can. If you join our church you can have the new wine *and* the new wineskin." At its face value, it looks very plausible and some have been attracted to it. Actually, it is a misinterpretation of what Jesus was teaching. New churches cannot be justified on the basis of these verses.

When I left school in 1950, my father sent me out to Bordeaux in France to learn the wine trade. It helped me later to understand the meaning of this passage and to know that the popular interpretation I have mentioned is wrong. How should we interpret what Jesus said?

There are five main lessons we can learn from this passage.

1) *We must not put new wine into old wineskins*

Jesus made it clear, "no one puts new wine into old wineskins." It is obviously a mistake to do so. Wine goes through a natural process called "fermentation." During this process, it expands as it ferments and puts considerable strain on whatever contains it. In Jesus' day, it was skins; when I worked in the wine cellars of Bordeaux, it was wooden barrels. The barrels had to be pliable, for the expansion of the gases in the fermenting process made this essential. I remember seeing these barrels almost bursting because of the tremendous pressure brought to bear on them.

If you are foolish enough to put new wine into old wineskins, you will in fact lose both. The skins will burst and the wine will be spilt.

Renewal movements, especially at their outset, are heady stuff. There is plenty of enthusiasm. People want to go places. Worship becomes emotional and free, services are extended. New ministries develop and Christians become much more dedicated and committed to serve the Lord and the Church. It is as foolish to thrust this immediately and without reserve into the staid setting of most of our churches as it is to put the new wine into old wineskins. Such a

Fresh Not New Wineskins

confrontation can only prove mutually destructive. Both the wine and the wineskin will be lost.

2) *We must put new wine into wineskins*

If it is foolish to put new wine into old wineskins, it is just as foolish not to put new wine into skins at all. It can't exist on its own, it has to be contained. The natural process of fermentation needs to take place in something. In fact it won't take place on its own—only when it is suitably contained.

Equally, the new wine of the Spirit needs to be brought to maturity in the disciplined context of a body of people, who can guard it all from excesses and at the same time allow it the freedom it needs to go through the fermentation process.

3) *We must put new wine into fresh wineskins*

The RSV helps us here by using two different English words, "new" and "fresh," to translate two Greek words, *neos* and *kainos*. A better translation would be "renewed wineskins." The wine growers in Jesus' time did not put their new wine into new wineskins any more than the Bordeaux business I worked for put new wine into new barrels. That would have been very wasteful and expensive. Wineskins were used over and over again, sometimes being patched up and mended when they had been torn. We did the same in those Bordeaux cellars where I worked. But the old wineskins needed to be "freshened" or "renewed" to make them pliable to withstand the extra pressures of

THAT WE MAY BE ONE

fermentation. This was done simply by soaking them in water for several hours or even days.

So the new wine of the Spirit does not need completely new structures, certainly not new churches, but renewed people and churches to contain the new movement of God, with structures that are pliable enough to contain the new enthusiasm.

4) *We must realize that new wine is no good until it has matured*

When you have drunk old and mature wine, it spoils you for anything else. New wine is always poor (and more intoxicating) and needs to be matured for several years before it reaches its prime. "No one," Jesus said, "after drinking old wine desires new, for he says the old is good." Jesus is not necessarily saying this in a derogatory sense, although, as we shall see in a moment, there is that thought included in this verse. It is a fact of life that old wine is more palatable than new. But it is also true that all old wine was once new—and it could never have come to maturity without the process of fermentation.

It is equally obvious that new movements of the Holy Spirit in their early stages go through periods of immaturity. There is much froth and bubble. The church needs to be flexible enough to contain this. But the tendency to regard the new wine as superior to the old needs to be strenuously resisted. Pride and an elitist spirit, which often is linked with fanaticism and a judgmental attitude, are the classic symptoms of the

Fresh Not New Wineskins

sin which so easily besets all new movements.

5) *We must also realize that the new wine is to be received and accepted by the old*

There is, in the words of Jesus, at least some implication of smugness in the phrase "the old is good." It would be no good at all if the old wine questioned the new wine's right to exist on the grounds that the old is good and the new is bad. As we have said before, all old wine was once new and we should never forget it. The old should be as tolerant of the new (with all its excesses in fermentation) as the new should be of the old. They are in fact the same; the only difference lies in the fact that in the overall process of wine-making they are at different stages.

Of course, there are not exact parallels between the illustration Jesus gives us and the reality of our own experiences. Nevertheless it is well known that older people tend to react more negatively to new things than the young. They should not do so simply because something is new. Not all new things are bad. Some are good and need to be received as such. And if the new is a bit intoxicating, then it needs to be tolerated provided it is a part of the natural process of maturity—and indeed welcomed as wine which is on the way to becoming a good vintage.

The Two Covenants

But we need now to look at the context in which these words of Jesus were spoken. He compares His

THAT WE MAY BE ONE

own ministry with that of John the Baptist whose disciples often fasted and prayed, whereas His own disciples didn't. John was the last of the Old Testament prophets. But Jesus had come to inaugurate a new age, a completely new dispensation. Old things were going to pass away and all things were to become new. It was, in fact, to be a New Covenant. History itself was to be cleaved in two: everything before was to be called B.C. (Before Christ), everything after A.D. (*Anno Domini*). It was the turning point in history. Everything in the future was going to be different.

This was the new wine that Jesus was talking about, and quite clearly it could not be contained in the old wineskins of Judaism. The break-point was two-fold. In the first place, Jesus was the Messiah and had to be believed in and obeyed. He was God's Son incarnate. The old Judaism did not accommodate itself to that fact. Either He was what He claimed to be—or a religious fraud, and the Jews of Jesus' day had to make up their minds. To some He was their Messiah, but to many others He was a fraud. So God's blessings were now to be received through Jesus Christ. He was "the way, the truth and the life" and no one could come to the Father except through Him.

The second break-point came when Jesus and the early Church made it abundantly clear that God was no longer committed just to the Jewish people—in Christ there was no longer Jew or Greek—but we are all one in Christ Jesus. This was unacceptable to the Jews who were more anxious than ever to cling to their

Fresh Not New Wineskins

divine privileges. This comes out clearly in the story of Paul giving his testimony to the Jews in Jerusalem. The mob listened attentively to his Christian testimony until he told them that God had sent him to the Gentiles. We are told, "Up to this word they listened to him; then they lifted up their voices and said, 'Away with such a fellow from the earth, for he ought not to live.' "

So very soon there was a cleavage between the Jews and the new Christians, most of whom were converted Jews themselves. The new wine of the gospel had to have fresh wineskins, otherwise it would have burst the old wineskins and been spilt on the ground. The Christian Church was God's answer to this.

It is important for us, therefore, to realize that we cannot apply the same principle whenever there is a new renewal movement. It is a great temptation to do so. Certainly, as we shall see, most of the Church for fifteen hundred years did not interpret these verses in that way. What was justifiable in the case of the change-over from the Old to the New Covenant is not justifiable when it comes to new movements within the church. It is clear that the Old Covenant, which was only for Jews and based on the law and which was operative before the coming of God's Son Jesus Christ, could not co-exist with the New Covenant which was for all nations and races on the face of the earth, and was based on grace through the Cross of Christ. The New abrogated the Old, and the fresh wineskin, which for most of the earliest Christians was

THAT WE MAY BE ONE

Jewish in character, was the Church, the Body of Christ on earth. If that is true, then this reference to fresh wineskins cannot possibly justify the setting up of new churches every time the Spirit moves in power on the Church. The Church is one, just as the nation was one.

Then how did the Christian Church cope with renewal movements in the centuries after Christ's ascension? We need to turn to this matter next.

4
No Exclusives

It is a fact that most churches seem to have their "exclusives" and most church movements have had an exclusive wing to them. There are, for example, the Strict Baptists, who have rigid rules of church membership as opposed to Baptists who have a much more open approach. The nineteenth-century Plymouth Brethren soon split into two streams, the Open Brethren and the Exclusive Brethren. We have more recent examples of this. In the 1960s, the Evangelical world in Britain polarized into two camps. There were those who followed Dr. Martyn Lloyd-Jones and who said "enough is enough" regarding modern ecumenism. They felt the time had come to leave the historic churches, which they believed had hopelessly compromised the gospel, and form independent Evangelical churches. On the other hand, there were those who rallied around leaders like John Stott and organizations like the Evangelical Alliance and believed they were called to stay in their churches and reform them from within.

The same kind of schism has taken place in the Charismatic Renewal between some of the so-called

THAT WE MAY BE ONE

House Churches and those who have been renewed within the denominations. There are now exclusive Charismatics and open Charismatics. History has an unfortunate knack of repeating itself. The new reasons for division are different from the split in the Evangelical world, and indeed the charismatic divisions are splitting Evangelical churches. But the results are unfortunate. Why does this happen over and over again? What lies behind the exclusive or elitist approach?

I am convinced that one of the main reasons is the lack of a clear grasp of scriptural principles of unity. Many do not understand that the same problems had to be faced in the early days of the Church, and that Paul and others regarded all forms of elitism or exclusiveness as sinful—an offense to Christ, who is the Head of the Church, and to one's fellow Christians, who are its members. There were some who tried to be "exclusives" in the early Church, but they were condemned for their actions by the apostle Paul, who regarded the principle of comprehensiveness and tolerance as something worth fighting for, knowing that all forms of exclusiveness would ultimately weaken and divide the Church in an unacceptable manner.

We are fortunate to have a great deal of information about the problems the early Christians had to face to help us understand how they coped with the difficulties of controversy and managed to maintain the unity of the Church at the same time. The major problem,

No Exclusives

which acted as a catalyst, was the relationship between the Jewish and Gentile Christians and whether or not the law should continue to apply to Jewish Christians and be extended to include the Gentiles.

In Galatians 2 we have a personal account of the way in which Paul confronted Peter on this issue. Peter had traveled to Antioch and was very happy to eat and have fellowship with the many non-Jewish Christians in that city. But then a party who were "exclusives" arrived in the city, whereupon Peter "separated himself, fearing the circumcision party" (v. 12). Peter had set a bad example and was apparently soon followed by the rest of the Jewish Christians. Even Barnabas was "carried away by their insincerity" (v. 13). Paul regarded this as being "not straightforward about the truth of the gospel" and opposed Peter to his face.

So we see Paul opposing the spirit of exclusiveness. He had experienced many problems with the circumcision party, but at no point does he argue that they should be excluded from the Church. For Paul, the Church should be comprehensive enough to include both viewpoints. What he does oppose is the attempt by some of the Jewish Christians to withdraw fellowship from the Gentile Christians.

Paul wanted to see this controversey worked out inside the Church, not outside it. He was as aware as anyone of the tensions which this controversy brought. He was strongly opposed to the so-called Judaizers,

THAT WE MAY BE ONE

believing that they were compromising vital gospel principles. In this same epistle, he says in one place that he wishes they would castrate themselves (5:12)! But never does he attempt to unchurch them, and he cooperated fully in the Jerusalem Council, which was convened to try to settle this particular controversy. Paul submitted to the decisions of that Council, although he could not have been wholly happy with them, implying as they do some measure of compromise.

Jesus Was Not an Exclusive

What Paul was struggling for was the continuation within the Church of the spirit of his Lord and Master, Jesus Christ. Jesus was not an exclusive. It is true that He was called by the Father to minister only to "the lost sheep of the house of Israel." It is true, too, that He gave an impression of being exclusive when He said to the Canaanite woman, "it is not fair to take the children's bread and throw it to the dogs" (Matt. 15:26). But even then He went on to heal this woman's daughter. He also healed the Centurion's slave and spoke prophetically about the inclusiveness of the future people of God. As John comments about the death of Jesus, it was "for the nation and not for the nation only, but to gather into one the children of God who are scattered abroad" (John 11:52). Paul re-echoes this thought when he writes in Ephesians about the blood of Christ making peace between the Jew and the Gentile, "for he is our peace, who has made us

No Exclusives

both one, and has broken down the dividing wall of hostility" (2:14).

Alas, Christians today build up again the "walls of hostility" which Jesus radically demolished at Calvary. The Temple in Jesus' day was divided into sections; there was a part of it into which only Jews were allowed to go. Women were prevented from entering another part. Even God had His exclusive area. But Jesus' death tore down even the curtain which separated God from His people. No-go areas were now non-existent. But we have re-erected these barriers. There are barriers between Catholics and Protestants, between Evangelicals and Liberals, and now between Charismatics and non-Charismatics and varieties of Charismatics.

Those who take the view that the Church should be "pure" and only composed of "born-again" Christians, should look closely at the attitude of Jesus to His disciples. Their relationship to Him was a distinctly patchy affair. They blew alternately hot and cold. They were not exactly full of faith. They were, in Jesus' own words, "slow of heart to believe." One of them was working against Jesus, eventually selling Him to the rulers of the Jews for money. One was to deny Him three times: "I never knew the man." They were all to forsake Him and run away, leaving Him in the hands of His enemies. But Jesus, although He rebuked them frequently, never rejected them. He did not even excommunicate Judas Iscariot, giving him every opportunity of repenting right up to the last minute. Judas left the apostolic band of his own volition.

THAT WE MAY BE ONE

God's people have always been a mixed company. Certainly the disciples of Christ were. But Jesus put up with them. Why is it that some of God's people have always felt it their duty to draw the lines narrower than God does? Why is it that some Christians reject, those whom God accepts? An ingredient of the exclusive spirit is often human pride and Jesus told a number of parables to expose it. The most famous is the one about a father who had two sons. The father's love *included* the prodigal, but the elder brother's pride *excluded* him. Then there were the two men who went into the Temple to pray, the one smugly self-satisfied and looking down his nose at the tax collector alongside him. But it was the humble prayer of the tax collector which was answered and he went home forgiven. Quite obviously Jesus abhorred this proud spirit which excluded others and condemned them. We are not to compare ourselves with one another. We shall always find someone else whom we deem less spiritual than ourselves. We are self-deceived when we elevate ourselves at the expense of others.

When we turn to the letters of Paul to the Corinthians, we see mirrored in them a far from spiritual Church. Here was a church which was having difficulties with the doctrine of the Resurrection! The inference was that some of them did not believe in it, or if they did they had got it distorted. And look what was going on in the church! There was unabashed incest; there was pandemonium in worship; there was drunkenness at Holy Communion and there was charismatic bedlam.

No Exclusives

Yet never once does Paul attempt to unchurch them. *Far from it: he tells them quite clearly that they are "the Body of Christ."* Nor does he advise the sound and committed Christians amongst them to form a renewed Church. No, he corrects the abuses and teaches them the truth. He calls on them to repent (which it would seem they did to some extent). Those who are looking today for "pure" renewed churches without any "unrenewed" element, are going beyond the mandate of Paul and, therefore, of scripture.

There is something that sounds very spiritual when we postulate the Church as composed only of Charismatics, or committed Christians, or people who agree with us about most matters of theological difference. But these sorts of Churches have seldom existed even in the earliest period of the Church.

But Paul had another problem on his hands— charismatic exclusiveness. These Christians in Corinth had become unbalanced in their pursuit of the miraculous. They even expressed their criticism of Paul because, according to their judgment, he was not charismatic enough. They were strong on charismatic gifts but not on the development of Christian character. They became proud of their spiritual achievements and revelations of God. As we have already pointed out, exclusiveness arises out of spiritual pride, and that lay behind their rejection of Paul. The words Paul uses to describe these Charismatics are "superlative apostles" (see 2 Cor. 11:5, 12), and he makes it plain that he does not regard himself

THAT WE MAY BE ONE

as inferior to them at all. But he also clearly states that he regards these exclusives as "false apostles, deceitful workmen, disguising themselves as apostles of Christ" (2 Cor. 11:13).

Unfortunately we have not seen the last of these "superlative apostles"—arrogant Charismatics who boast of their spiritual achievements and condemn those whom they believe are lacking the gifts they think they ought to have. Paul is as concerned to reject this form of exclusiveness as he is the legalistic form. Both puff men up and give them a false sense of their importance. Both promote exclusiveness and cause division in the Body of Christ. They separate certain kinds of people from others and encourage judgmental attitudes, and narrowness of vision.

New Testament Churches?

Some people today claim to belong to a "New Testament Church." What they mean by this is that their church is run on New Testament Church lines. They believe that the New Testament supplies us with a blueprint which Jesus Christ intended the Church to follow. They see their own church and its pattern of ministry, worship and life conforming to the blueprint. So they feel they are justified in calling themselves a "New Testament Church."

One is tempted to ask, "Which New Testament Church?" Is it like the Corinthian church, which we have just described? Or is it like one of the churches to which Jesus Christ himself addressed His "letters" in

No Exclusives

Revelation 2-3? How about the church at Thyatira where there is a prophetess seducing the men? Or the church in Sardis which has a name of being alive, but is dead? Or the church in Laodicea outside the door of which Christ stands and knocks, a church which, like the water which ran by the city, is neither hot nor cold?

None of these churches would measure up to the standards which some today expect of "New Testament Churches." Yet both Jesus Christ and the apostle Paul called these fellowships "churches." They did not unchurch their members in spite of the dreadful things that were being done within them.

But what is even more important to notice is that Jesus never in His remarks to these churches calls upon the faithful to leave them and start new pure churches. He says to the remnant in Thyatira, "Hold fast what you have, until I come" (2:25). To the faithful believers in Philadelphia He writes, "Hold fast what you have, so that no one may seize your crowns" (3:11). Nowhere in the New Testament is there a call to a spiritual elite to forsake a dead or compromising church and start a new one. In fact such a move is anathema to the Spirit of God. In John's First Epistle, he describes some who had gone out from the church. This proved "they were not of us; for if they had been of us, they would have continued with us; but they went out, that it might be plain that they all are not of us" (1 John 2:19). In New Testament times, those who left the churches were regarded as false brethren, because the natural attitude of Christians was to

THAT WE MAY BE ONE

continue within the Church even when many within it had compromised the faith by their false teaching, immoral behavior or half-hearted commitment.

The fact of the matter is that there is no blueprint for the Church, even for the earliest and the first-established churches. Nowhere in the New Testament are there mandatory statements about how the Church should be governed, what officers it should have, how its worship should be regulated, etc. There was an abundance of variation from earliest days and the Holy Spirit delighted to inspire many different kinds of churches. Jesus Christ himself said very little about the Church and laid down no pattern to govern its life. It was meant to develop naturally and spontaneously, and to be flexible enough to adjust to the many different situations in which it found itself in those early days.

There is no such thing as a "New Testament Church," but a whole series of different churches in New Testament days, no one of which is held up as *the* example for all succeeding generations to follow.

Come Out from Among Them?

But does not the Bible somewhere say that we are to "come out from among them" and is there not, therefore, a biblical principle that when things get very bad we become guilty by association if we continue as members of such a church?

Well, there is a verse which says this, but like other verses it has often been misunderstood and made to

No Exclusives

apply to situations which it was never intended to relate to. It is an Old Testament quotation which Paul uses in 2 Corinthians 6:14-18. It is a call to separation *from the world* not from a back-slidden or unrenewed church. It is a call to forsake partnerships and liaisons with unrighteous people, people who are in league with Satan, worshipers of idols and unbelievers. It is a call to Christian commitment which inevitably involves us in a renunciation of the world, as our baptismal promises made abundantly plain. The "coming out" is from the world, not from the Church.

Of course some will argue, "What happens when the Church is invaded by the world so that it becomes indistinguishable from it?" Well, then it ceases to be "the Church" and becomes the world. But we should not apply this scripture normally to the Church, however unrenewed it may appear to be. God has not given us the task of judging the Church. The call to separation is always from the world, *never* from the Church.

I Have Need of You

Perfectionism has always proved the most subtle and dangerous of temptations for Christians. It seems such an admirable aspiration. And so it is—provided one never claims to have attained it. There have been those in the past who have claimed a kind of "sinless perfection." They have believed it possible to attain to a state of life in which they cease from sin. They become perfect in Christ. There have always been

THAT WE MAY BE ONE

Christians, like John Wesley, who have seemed to teach this. Actually they have often been misrepresented. They never taught in an absolute sense. They raised the sights of Christians to an entirely new level of expectation, without ever claiming to be perfect. They believed, rightly, that it was not God's will that men and women should constantly wallow in their sins, but by the grace of God they could attain to a state of sanctification which lifted them above and out of their sins.

But we are now having to face another form of perfectionism based on a misunderstanding of the New Testament and God's purpose for His people. It is a kind of church perfectionism. Of course, no one actually believes that there is a perfect church on earth. But there are some who believe that there is an absolute Bible pattern for the Church and that we are bound to conform to it if we are to be obedient to the Lord. And if we are not a part of such a church, then we should leave where we are and join this other kind of church. By implication the historic churches are so hopelessly compromised that to be part of any of them is to be contaminated. Such people argue that God's will cannot be fully done while we are members of such churches.

I believe this is wrong teaching, which we will not really find in the New Testament, which, as we have already seen, describes a whole variety of churches, which were in part weak, sinful, heretical and disobedient. They needed constantly to be corrected and

No Exclusives

censured by the apostles and by Jesus Christ himself. Succeeding history, as we shall see, produced even worse examples of churches which at times became hopelessly compromised by the world, the flesh and the devil. But the call to "leave the churches" was never given by Jesus Christ, the apostles or their successors. As time went on some did leave, although on the whole they were few in number. Although benefits did accrue initially to some of the groups which left the main body of the Church, in most instances the ultimate state of the new groups became worse than the church they were meant to reform or renew. The New Testament explicitly or implicitly requires church members to stay where they are and bloom where they have been planted, however unspiritual the rest of the church may seem to be.

5
The Two Structures

We can summarize the problems we are addressing in this book by posing this basic question: how does one deal with the situation in the Church when spiritual decline sets in? When all is light and love and freedom the Church has to handle a different set of problems. But what happens when God's people lapse into faithlessness, when worship becomes sterile and when the Church ceases to move forward in its evangelistic task? We soon realize when we look at the Old and New Testaments that this was a perennial problem. No sooner had the Israelites gained their great victory at Jericho, than they had to face humiliating defeat at Ai. The story of Israel is a see-saw business from beginning to end. One moment there was good leadership and righteousness pervaded the scene; next moment there was a period of spiritual decline and a lapse into idolatry.

We have tried to show how God dealt with these situations as they arose. How He did not ask anyone to separate from the unfaithful element in the nation and build a new righteous nation. God worked through faithful remnants—often groups of people, who, while

THAT WE MAY BE ONE

remaining in the nation, turned to God and through prayer and prophecy brought God's word to the nation until it repented and turned back to Him. In 2 Kings 19:30-31 there is a classic statement of this principle; "and the surviving remnant of the houses of Judah shall again take root downward, and bear fruit upward; for out of Jerusalem shall go forth a remnant, and out of Mount Zion a band of survivors. The zeal of the Lord will do this." God was going to preserve His people in the midst of all their troubles. It was a theme that the prophets turned to again and again. Isaiah speaks about "the remnants of Israel and the survivors of the house of Jacob" that will return to their God (10:20-21). Jeremiah refers to "the remnant of God's flock" that He will gather from all the countries where He has driven them (23:3). Micah speaks of God gathering the remnant of Israel (2:12). Zechariah declares that God will cause the remnant of the people to possess the land (8:12).

The prophets also saw it like a huge tree that had been cut down, leaving only an old stump in the ground. Isaiah calls this "the stump of Jesse' (11:1), and prophesies that from that stump there would come forth a shoot and a branch would grow out of its roots. This would be the Messiah, and the Spirit of the Lord would rest upon him and his delight would be in the fear of the Lord (vv. 2-3).

God has never left himself without witnesses. There has always been a faithful remnant—and out of that old stump has grown the new tree. The history of the

The Two Structures

Church from the first century onward is the story of the vital interplay between two different kinds of structures. The Church was to go on experiencing renewal after renewal *without splitting the Church into renewed and unrenewed members.* The Church remained one and, with a few exceptions, was able to handle its militants without division. It was also able to expand and eventually preach the gospel throughout the whole of Europe and in later centuries throughout the entire world because it managed to handle this sort of situation with skill and tolerance. Thus the "hot" remnant was able to function within the Church, which itself was constantly in a state of flux—often going through periods of spiritual decline—lapsing into the most irreligious, even licentious, behavior. It was not until the Reformation that, as we have already mentioned, open schism was tolerated. But that is another story which we must turn to later.

How was all this possible? It seems that only one answer can be given: that from New Testament times onward the Church increasingly recognized not one but two kinds of church structure. For want of a better way of describing these two structures, let's call them "the inclusive" and "the exclusive," although we must be swift to explain that we are using the word "exclusive" differently from its use in the previous chapter. There we saw that exclusive Christianity, when one group of Christians separate themselves from other Christians because they want to preserve a certain kind of purity, is condemned by Paul as anathema to the gospel of God's grace, for God has already made us one in Christ. In that case, the exclusiveness was racial. The issue concerned the relationship between Jews and Gentiles. Paul regarded it as a form of exclusiveness which must not be tolerated in the Christian Church. But in this chapter I want to use the word in a good sense. Perhaps the best way of showing the difference is by describing part of the ministry of Paul himself.

Paul and Barnabas were members of the large church in Antioch. Its structure was inclusive. It would have included within its membership many different kinds of people—adults and children, Jews and Gentiles, soldiers and civilians, rich and poor, dedicated and half-hearted Christians. From that mixed fellowship God called Paul and Barnabas for an outreach ministry (see Acts 13), which was to be a prototype of another kind of structure, which I am calling "exclusive." It was exclusive in the sense that not every member of the church in Antioch belonged to it. But it was still part of that church, and there was a continuing, loving and cordial relationship between them. The difference between the two structures was one of *function.* Paul's missionary band was something else, something different. But it was not another or separate "church." It was simply a body of people who were committed to a function which related closely to the home base; it was a commitment beyond the more varied forms of Christian discipleship that existed in that church.

The Two Structures

For the next fifteen hundred years, in fact three times longer than the period from the Reformation until now, the Western Church was to continue largely as a united body, apart from a few minor schisms, because it recognized these two structures, which I have called the inclusive and the exclusive, and because it saw them as complementing, not competing with each other. The exclusive groups had a special function which related to the larger and inclusive body. They were there to serve the inclusive body, not to condemn it. There was still one body, but two different kinds of structures within that one body.

There were two main functions which the exclusive structures served. The first, of which Paul's apostolic bands are a good example, was for the evangelization of the world. We must always remember that most of the evangelization of the world was carried out from the first century onwards by exclusive structures, groups of people committed to this one task. Prior to the Reformation, they were mostly members of religious orders, monks who traveled all over Europe preaching the gospel and founding churches. Good examples were the Celtic monks who evangelized Western and even Central Europe. Subsequent to the Reformation, this work has continued to be done by monks and nuns of the Roman Catholic Church and in the Protestant world by missionary societies.

But there was another function which these exclusive groups had, the renewal of the Church. The beginnings of monasticism can be traced to this

THAT WE MAY BE ONE

function rather than the missionary. The first religious orders were groups of Christians who were dissatisfied with the spiritual condition of the Church and wanted to see it restored to what they were convinced it should be. They wanted the freedom to live that life themselves, even if no one else saw the importance of it. They read the New Testament and realized that the church of their day no longer possessed the enthusiasm of those early Christians and their dedication to the Lord. So they believed that they should make another commitment beyond that of their baptism promises. Eventually this developed into vows of poverty, chastity and obedience. They wanted to re-discover the springs of true Christianity and live a life as fully pleasing to the Lord as was possible; and for this to happen they needed to separate themselves fully from the world (and to some extent from much of the existing Church) and give themselves totally to God.

So we see that for hundreds of years both evangelism and renewal were sustained by these exclusive groups of people. They were not new "churches," for there could be only one Church. They were not in competition with the inclusive structures—which were, indeed, flexible enough to include them. There were times of friction between them. But on the whole they related well together, the exclusive religious orders seeing that part of their role was to serve the larger Church. When the Church's spiritual life declined, there were always those who were "survivors," or a

The Two Structures

faithful remnant who sustained the Church by their extra dedication. The work of evangelism, which was often dangerous and required extra physical as well as spiritual qualities, was ideally suited to these exclusive groups. The Church militant here on earth needed, as modern armies do, extraordinary regiments, like commando units or the S.A.S. (Specialty Air Service), to fulfill the difficult task of planting churches where the gospel had not previously been preached.

Many Protestants are prejudiced when it comes to the part that religious orders have played in the history of the Church. Those who say, "All we need is the Bible," often do not realize that we owe it to the religious orders that we have a Bible at all, for the sacred texts came down to us copied faithfully by monks. We forget that the western world was largely evangelized by these same people—at the cost of thousands of lives.

It is no exaggeration to say that the cause of Christ for hundreds of years depended more on these men than on any other single factor. They banded themselves together into communities, feeling called to another commitment, which distinguished them from the rest of the Church. They were certainly part of the Church. They were not a superior group, only a different group. The Church has never been divided, at least in God's sight, into first and second-class Christians. Some are called to a special vocation of separation from the world, whereas the majority of God's people are called to a special vocation of

THAT WE MAY BE ONE

involvement in the world. Both are necessary and complementary to each other.

Reformation Changes Things

Now we need to look at what happened at the Reformation. The Protestant Reformers reacted against the religious orders. It is true that some had become corrupted by power, and had lost their former spiritual life and vision. We need to remember that Martin Luther was a monk before he became a Protestant leader. But the reaction of the Reformers meant that the two types of structure were no longer acceptable to Protestants. They were replaced by the one inclusive type—the State Church. However, that was not the whole story. There were others who were pioneering another type of church structure—the Anabaptists. There were many groups under this general heading, and this type of church developed into many more forms in the coming centuries. We would include amongst them the Baptists, Congregationalists, Quakers, Mennonites, Hutterites and later groups like the Salvation Army and the Pentecostals. They have typified the desire for a "pure" Church—what is often called a "gathered" Church. In a sense they stand mid-way between the inclusive and the exclusive. They were to react strongly to the State churches, and became involved in open conflict with the Reformers and the State itself, many of their members being imprisoned for their convictions and

The Two Structures

some dying as a result of the persecution they received.

But very soon the State church inclusive type of structure proved wholly inadequate to cope with the spiritual life of its members. As the fervor of the Reformation declined and dryness set in, there was a demand for spiritual renewal. Amongst Lutherans this desire was given expression by the so-called Pietists, and amongst Angelicans by the Methodists. In the eighteenth and nineteenth centuries, revivals broke out at regular intervals, great movements of spiritual life designed to restore the churches to whole-hearted commitment to Christ and the power of the Holy Spirit. The Roman Catholic Church also had similar movements, as, indeed, did Eastern Orthodoxy in this period. The more inclusive the Church was, the more capable it seems to have been to handle the renewal movements and keep them within its borders for its own benefit, and the benefit of the renewal itself. The Eastern Orthodox Church, the Roman Catholic Church and the Lutherans largely succeeded in this; Anglicans partly succeeded; but the Free churches had more failures. The revival movement of the eighteenth century in Britain, led by Anglicans like George Whitefield and the Wesleys, remained partly in the Church and partly outside, and it gave birth to a new denomination, the Methodists. But the Free churches in the same period suffered frequent schisms through confrontation with these renewal movements. The Plymouth Brethren (although their early leaders

THAT WE MAY BE ONE

were largely former Anglicans), the Salvation Army, the Holiness Churches and the Pentecostals drew their new members largely from the Free Churches.

Our Own Situation

What we have just shared applies just as much to our own present situation. I want now to try to summarize what I have written and apply it to what we see at the present time.

1) *The historical perspective*

We always have to be careful when we are interpreting history. It is so easy to be selective in such a way as to distort the facts. History is never as neat and tidy as some of us would wish. There always have been splinter groups in the Church, some of whom have separated themselves from the main body of believers. The quest for a "pure" and scriptural church has continued all through the centuries. I would not want to give the impression that the two different types of church were universally accepted. There was often deep tension between the inclusive and exclusive types of structure. At the same time, there have always been independent-type churches that cannot be fitted into either of these categories. They were to proliferate at the time of the Reformation and received bad treatment from the Reformers. The modern house church movement is another in this succession of "dissenters" that stretch back down the centuries. We must not underestimate the tensions there have been

The Two Structures

in the Church from the beginning. It will help us to understand what is happening in the church body if we recognize that it has happened frequently in the past and we realize that there are no slick answers to these problems.

2) *The divine perspective*

It would seem that God has chosen to bless and, therefore, to recognize and use both these kinds of structures and both these kinds of churches. Of course it is important to have a structure for our churches in which God's people can function properly and live a life of obedience to the Lord himself. It must also be admitted that there are churches which are so traditional and conservative in their attitudes that it is virtually impossible for a person to live the kind of Christian life he wants to. But the point I want to make is that God does not seem to require of us only one of these kinds of structures, but is able to use both of them, albeit differently. I would guess that the divine perspective is such that God rejoices in the variety of expressions of divine grace and is very much more open and tolerant than many of us.

3) *The practical perspective*

The house churches in Britain now constitute the largest new kind of church since the Pentecostal Movement began in the early part of this century. Their name is an unfortunate misnomer, since, though many still do meet and worship in their homes, they

THAT WE MAY BE ONE

are not particularly tied to domestic meeting places, nor is the use of them a matter of strict dogma in these churches. Some meet in secular buildings (town-halls, etc.), others are now buying redundant church property.

It is to be regretted that there should need to be yet another denomination, as if we did not have enough. But it would be unjust to blame this entirely on the house churches. Many churches have been neglectful of their members, or fed them on an unhealthy diet. Can one wonder when people, especially the younger ones, leave their churches and join one of the new, lively house churches?

This book has been deliberately written with a view to helping each side of the divide to understand the other better, and to encourage not only forbearance but mutual acceptance, respect and cooperation.

Perhaps I could end by giving a practical illustration of the point that I am making. We live in a small town in Sussex, the population of which has grown considerably since the Second World War. In this town, there is a lively house church, several Anglican churches, some of which are experiencing renewal, a Roman Catholic church and a number of Free churches. The Lord has given to all of us, as Christians, the responsibility of being witnesses in this town. How are people going to be reached? I am quite certain there is a large number of people who have never had any allegiance to any church before; they are not believers, but the important point I want to make is that they are

The Two Structures

not lapsed Catholics or Anglicans or Methodists. They have never belonged anywhere, and have at the moment no intention of belonging to any church. It is to these people that the house church can have an evangelistic ministry which the other churches have much less hope of reaching.

At the same time, there are large numbers of people who are lapsed church members. They may have been baptized and had some Christian influence in their schooling. They may go to church very occasionally, particularly at Christmas. These kinds of people are less likely to be reached by the new house churches; if the historic churches are doing their work properly, they can have a fruitful time with these people.

If this is true, cannot these two different kinds of churches cooperate together at least in this task? Why should we be in direct competition with one another, doing our own thing as if the other churches didn't exist. There are other ways, too, in which cooperation can take place to the mutual benefit of all concerned, and, what is even more important, to the glory of God.

In some ways, our present situation is more confusing than at any time since the first century. Therefore, it is more important than ever that we think clearly about these matters and prevent, as far as possible, Christians forming their own camps and separating themselves from one another. The call to unity is not a matter of choice; it is a divine imperative which we must obey.

6

Handling Our Differences

The words of Jesus and the documents of the New Testament suggest that one of the facts of Christian life is that God's people will always have their differences, and, therefore, if they are to enjoy the unity of the Holy Spirit, they need to discover ways in which they can live together with these differences unresolved, without each side accusing the other of compromise. We have to learn to live with people with whom we disagree without feeling guilty about it, and without feeling that we are to be their judges.

For hundreds of years, the Christian Church has been subjected to a process of fragmentation which has caused much grief to the Lord Jesus Christ, provided a stumbling block to millions of unbelievers, divided families and friends and provoked anger and bitterness between Christians. If the Church had spent less time on its own internal strife and more time on making common cause against its enemies, the Kingdom of God would have been extended much further and the world would have become a better place. The Church as a whole, and we as its members, need to learn a great deal about the art of handling differences.

THAT WE MAY BE ONE

Acknowledging Differences

The first hurdle to jump is to face up to the fact that while we live in this world and are limited by our imperfect humanity there are bound to be differences between Christians on a wide range of subjects. This will not only be true in areas of debate such as unilateralism and the bomb, but also in areas like baptism and its practice, the Second Coming, charismatic gifts and the experience of the Holy Spirit. Seemingly equally devout and committed Christians may well vary considerably in their viewpoints. While we are in the flesh, we shall always be "seeing through a glass darkly." Only when we are all face to face with Jesus Christ will our differences be resolved—and by then they won't matter much anyway. We should, therefore, be careful about registering shock or sorrow over differences (which imply that they ought not to exist because we have got the truth). We will guard our language and avoid words and phrases like "it is evident" (when it is not to some), "clearly" (when the issues can easily be foggy), and "obviously" (when for some it is far from obvious). We must never assume that everyone thinks as we do, and we need to remember that some of our differences are more to do with the language we use than anything else. We should never be surprised when we realize that some Christians see things differently from ourselves; and it is not helpful when our instinct is to assume that they are blind leaders of the blind, stubborn or willfully disobedient. We may well end up finding that they

Handling Our Differences

were right and we were wrong. Though we should make every effort to resolve our differences (though being careful not to major on trivial disagreements), sadly we must accept the fact that we shall pass through the pearly gates with many of them still unresolved. It may be that for some there is no need to find agreement, for truth sometimes lies in *both* rather than in one or the other proposition. We are wasting our time trying to reconcile friends. In other cases, *both* of us may be wrong. But whatever is the truth of the matter, differences will exist between Christians until Jesus comes again.

It follows, therefore, that one or the other of the parties to a dispute has to compromise for the sake of unity. It is as impossible for Christians to dwell together in unity in the Church without some compromises, as it is for a husband and wife to live together in a marriage. Only perfect and infallible people can insist that they are right and all other contrary opinions are wrong. And since such people do not exist, the situation can never arise. In fact the only such person to live on this earth, our Lord Jesus Christ, had to live a life of some compromise himself. He was part of a corrupt society, yet played His own part in it "obeying Caesar." He identified with unspiritual synagogues and submitted to their leaders. This shows that it is possible to have a heart and will of uncompromising commitment to God while at the same time, for other reasons, having to compromise in

THAT WE MAY BE ONE

some of the affairs of men. While we live on this imperfect planet, we are bound to have compromise in some way or another.

Biblical Principles

It is important to notice that the New Testament also acknowledges that there will be differences between Christians. There is no book of Leviticus in the New Testament, laying down hard and fast rules and regulations. This is especially true of church government, which has been in the past fertile ground for disagreements between Christians. There is no uniform system laid down as a matter of principle, and the churches today reflect (quite rightly) many of these different approaches. It is a pity that so many churches in the past have been dogmatic when the New Testament churches tolerated much variety.

In Romans 14 Paul develops important principles of toleration, especially for the person whom he calls "weak in faith." It is a sad commentary today that some so-called modern "New Testament Churches" don't *welcome,* as Paul urged the Romans to do (v. 1), such people as members of the Church. Reading between the lines in this chapter, we realize that these early churches had many different opinions about things. Paul does not always come down on one side or the other. He urges toleration and a sense of proportion. The Kingdom of God is not primarily concerned with side issues but with "righteousness and peace and joy in the Holy Spirit" (v. 17).

Handling Our Differences

He goes on to urge the Christians in Rome to "pursue what makes for peace and for mutual upbuilding." There are numerous occasions when Christians who agree fundamentally on major issues are torn apart by comparatively unimportant differences. This is sad. Paul returns to the same theme in Colossians 2:16, where the readers had obviously lost a sense of proportion. Some of them had been "disqualifying" (excommunicating?) people and "taking a stand" on issues for which there ought to have been mutual toleration. Paul urges them to "hold fast to the Head." We shall return to look more closely at Romans 14 in the next chapter.

Limits to Toleration

One of the difficulties we have to face is that there may well be a difference of opinion as to what constitutes primary and secondary issues. What may be primary to one person may be secondary to another. For some Baptist believers, baptism by total immersion is primary, while for some Pentecostals, Spirit baptism and the initial evidence of speaking in tongues is primary. In both cases, the majority of Christians would not regard these doctrines as primary. Here, too, there is a need for mutual toleration and understanding. However, there are issues, which Paul mentions in his letters, which do not lie within the bounds of toleration. There were, for example, those who were preaching "another gospel" —though even here Paul does not put his personal

THAT WE MAY BE ONE

anathema on them. "Let him be accursed" is the furthest he is prepared to go (Gal. 1:7-9). The early church leaders were not as trigger-happy as some modern exponents of church discipline are. For instance, the apostle John mentions critically a man called Diotrephes who apparently was over-zealous in his disciplining of people, "putting them out of the church" (3 John 9). John assures his readers that if he is able to visit them, he will sort this man out.

Toleration Is Divine

We are to be tolerant because God is tolerant. If, as seems clear, God allows differences (and even creates them), then we must also. On some major issues, if God had wanted everything to be clearer He surely would have looked after us differently. If God the Holy Spirit had a major influence on the formation and writing of the New Testament, and knew what was to happen in the future, it is surely a fair question to ask, "Why didn't He make things clearer?" It would only have needed a few verses to have settled for all time some of the major areas of Christian controversy. Is it not fair to deduce from this that we need to be as tolerant of one another as God seems to be towards us? God has made clear what is essential for man's salvation and his life of obedience and faith. But where God has not made things clear in His word, we should be open to different opinions from equally devout Christians. Is it ever right for us to be stricter and more dogmatic that God seems to have been? Is it ever right for us to claim to know with certainty the answers to some of the ambiguities of Scripture? And if it may be right under certain circumstances for ourselves, are we ever justified in holding so strongly to these interpretations that we divide ourselves from others? These are important questions for us to attempt to answer. The gravest danger is that we begin to act as "God" and dethrone Him from His position as Lord of all creation.

Divisions, Not Differences are Sinful

One of the best features of the twentieth-century church has been the overwhelming sense of guilt that Christians have had over their divisions. Munger has listed the three "humiliations of Jesus." The first two are well-known: His incarnation and His crucifixion. But the third he calls "the divided state of the Church." Paul even relates this to a local situation. For example, the church in Corinth was divided by party strife, although still one body. "Is Christ divided?" he asked them (1 Cor. 1:13). If that question was relevant in a local church situation, where there was dissension and quarreling, how much more appropriate are these words when we look at the continuing divisions in the Body of Christ. One hesitates to speculate on what Paul would say to us, but he surely would address us all with considerable severity.

It is worth noticing that sins relating to division figure prominently in Paul's list of the works of the flesh (Gal. 5:19-21). Over half of them, in fact, have to do with this

THAT WE MAY BE ONE

subject. It is important to ponder the relationship between theological differences and ethical behavior. How many differences between Christians really come from genuine theological difficulties and how many from envy, jealousy, selfishness or a narrow party spirit? I would guess that most are a mixture of the two, but that the "flesh," in other words our sinful human nature, plays a greater part in theological differences than most of us are prepared to admit. If this is true, then the pathway to unity must route itself through repentance as well as dialogue and discussion. Paul actually accuses some in his day of preaching Christ "from envy and rivalry . . . and out of partisanship" (Phil. 1:15, 17). In 1 Timothy 6:4 ff. there is also a reference to those who have "a morbid craving for controversy and for disputes about words, which produce envy, dissension, slander, base suspicions and wrangling among men . . ." In most disputes there are some psychological overtones, in others there may be more serious psychological reasons for them and we should not close our minds to these possibilities.

We should face this issue seriously, as we are all too prone to make excuses for our divisions. *I believe all divisions in the Body of Christ are sinful.* It is perfectly true that some fellowships of believers grow in numbers and spiritual power to a point at which they have to divide if they are to grow further. That is healthy growth. There may be sound reasons why one group or body may deem it necessary to divide into two or more bodies. Provided this is done by agreement from both sides, it is not sinful. In fact, it may be sinful if they continue together. But whenever there is division which follows controversy and contention in a fellowship of God's people, where there is not a mutuality of agreement, then it is sinful and there will need to be a mutual repentance and reconciliation between those two bodies. The majority of divisions in the Body of Christ are of this unhealthy kind.

Handling Our Differences

If differences are bound to exist within the Body of Christ and to have them is not sinful, then it is important that we not only recognize this fact but that we seek to handle these differences in the right way. It is possible that some of them, if handled properly, can be resolved. There are two approaches which should be carefully avoided. There are those, whom we have already noticed, who seem to thrive on controversy and are never happier than when in the thick of it. They are swift to point out all differences and set them up in order to knock them down again like skittles in a bowling alley. The opposite approach is to minimize or ignore genuine differences and even to pretend that they don't exist. Some people are naturally timid, while others follow the philosophy of peace at any price. They don't want an argument at all. They are not interested in contending for the truth. They would rather knock the contenders' heads together and leave it at that. Both these attitudes are unrealistic and both these kinds of people need to be gently but firmly corrected.

Principles in Dispute

1) *Commitment to Christian unity*

We need to be committed to Christian unity and to recognize its importance and that it is only attainable by the grace of God. *In one sense, Christian unity is the gift of God, already given,* and so it can only be received by faith, never attained by human means. God's will is that His people be one; God is, therefore, committed to supplying us all with the grace for that unity. Paul says in Ephesians that it is God's purpose "to unite all things in Christ" and "there is one body" (Eph. 1:10, 4:4). We should desire that unity with all our hearts.

2) *Accuracy of understanding*

We need to know accurately the positions held by people; often differences occur or become unnecessarily exaggerated because of the ignorance that people have of each other's views and opinions. It is natural for us to be definite and clear about what *we believe.* But we need also to listen carefully to what those who disagree with us say, and come to an accurate understanding of it. It is easy for us to distort the views of others, sometimes in order to establish our own position. Others can be tempted to adjust either the one position or the other in order to try to

Handling Our Differences

reach an easy agreement. But that will not help. We cannot resolve our differences if we don't know accurately what they are.

3) *Freedom from wrong attitudes*

We need to be cleansed from the sins which either cause division or frustrate all efforts to bring about unity and acceptance of each other. We need to humble ourselves and be delivered from the pride and vanity which often cloud the issues and make it more difficult for agreement to be reached. We need to be careful about our use of words, not using offensive language or moralizing about issues which put guilt upon those whom we disagree with. We should avoid resorting to sarcasm or being cynical. We should not accuse those who disagree with us of "compromise."

4) *Respect*

We need to respect the other person's position and integrity. We need to show that we appreciate them and that that person has a right to his opinion, even if it is very different from our own.

5) *Open to reason*

We need, to use the words of the Epistle of James, to be "open to reason" (3:17). It is no good for either of the parties coming to discuss a matter of disagreement with the proviso in their hearts (if not on their lips), "You will never convince me." Both need to be open to listen, as far as possible without fear or prejudice, to the other person, and be open to correction, however painful and difficult this may be.

6) *Above all—love*

Above all—let love prevail. When it does there is no room left for pride, envy, fear or a party spirit. We should love those we disagree with so much that we want them to be proved right (provided, of course, it really is right in God's sight).

The Place of Leadership

All of us are called to reconciliation. God took the initiative in order to effect our reconciliation with himself: "God was in Christ reconciling the world to himself." He then commits to us "the message of reconcilation" (2 Cor. 5:19). But we are also to seek, as much as possible, to live in peace and unity with all God's people. That will sometimes mean that we shall need to be His agents of reconciliation.

Christian leaders have in this matter an awesome responsibility. One of the main functions, for example, of bishops is to be a "focus of unity," but the same can also be said of all leaders, whether we see them singly or in terms of group leadership. If only Christian leaders had taken seriously the statement in 1 Timothy 3:3 that one of the qualifications of a leader is that he should not be "quarrelsome!" This theme is repeated in 2 Timothy 2:24: "the Lord's servant must not be quarrelsome but kindly to everyone, an apt teacher, forbearing, correcting his opponents with gentleness."

Handling Our Differences

Yes, even in New Testament times Christian leaders had "opponents." Christian leaders, in other words, should not be pugnacious or trigger-happy, ready to pick a quarrel with the first person who contradicts them and to argue the hind leg off a donkey. Such people are unfitted for leadership in the Body of Christ. There will always be a need for correction, but those who correct should also be open to correction themselves. The leader is not always right.

Leaders should be harmonizers in the Body of Christ. Thus differences, even if they are not reconciled at first, are never allowed to become something which can threaten both the unity and the stability of the Body of Christ.

7
Neither Slave Nor Free

The apostle Paul is often depicted as a narrow-minded bigot. I believe this is character assassination of the worst kind. In fact if we read his letters carefully and trace the story of his ministry accurately as it is recorded in the Acts of the Apostles, we shall, I think, come to a quite different conclusion. He certainly had strong opinions about many things. But his arguments again and again are for mutual toleration in matters of dispute. Of course we need to be careful to see that Paul's toleration extended only over areas of disputable territory. It would be irresponsible to apply it to primary areas, where Paul is often devastatingly dogmatic. The Church is not to tolerate incest for example, but to discipline Christians who indulge in it. Paul says clearly that those who deny the gospel and preach "another" are anathema. What then are these principles in Romans 14 and 15?

1) *All of us are entitled to our own convictions* (v. 5)

> *Let everyone be fully convinced in his own mind*

THAT WE MAY BE ONE

In the churches, there will always be people who have different convictions about the same issue. We need to recognize this and allow others the right to disagree and to hold to their own viewpoints. Ultimately the individual is responsible to God and to God alone for his conscientious convictions, and his fellow Christians must respect such, even when they seem absurd.

2) *None of us lives to himself* (v. 7)

> *None of us lives to himself, and none of us dies to himself*

This is the converse of the first principle. Paul balances the assertion that the individual is entitled to his own convictions with the complementary truth that no one can think or act independently either of God or of his fellow Christians. No Christian can ever be an "independent." We talk freely about "independent churches," but in one sense there is no such thing. No one church is ever independent of the rest of the Church. It is sinful for a church or a Christian individual to say to the rest of the Body of Christ, "I have no need of you" (1 Cor. 12:21). This principle runs strongly through the whole of Romans 14. In verse 15 for example, Paul says that if another Christian is being injured by your faithful and dogged "convictions," then you are not walking in love.

Neither Slave Nor Free

3) *We are not to judge or despise one another* (vv. 10-13)

> *Then let us no more pass judgment on one another*

It is easy for us, when we hold strong convictions, to condemn those with whom we disagree. What is almost worse is when we despise them or their views. In judging others, we are usurping the role that only God has. We are acting the part of God. Paul frequently makes this clear; we must leave judgment to God, "for we shall all stand before the judgment seat of God," where "each of us shall give account of himself to God." Here, too, Paul is echoing the words of Christ in the Sermon on the Mount, "judge not that you be not judged" (Matt. 7:1).

4) *Nothing is unclean in itself* (v. 14)

> *I know and am persuaded in the Lord Jesus that nothing is unclean in itself*

Here is a most important principle, but one which needs more explanation. The main issue at stake in Rome was the question of food. There were some, it would seem, in the church in Rome who were convinced vegetarians. They believed strongly that meat was actually "unclean," and that was why they did not eat it. Paul disagreed with them vigorously on this point. It is interesting that he says "in the Lord Jesus," which may mean that he was aware of Jesus' own teaching in Mark 7:14-23 in which the Lord makes very similar statements. Even if meat is offered to idols it does not become "unclean" because things do not have moral value. It is what people do with things or what they think about them which raises moral issues.

Let me give a practical example of this. Say we have a bust of George III on the mantelpiece. Morally it is quite innocent. But what if there is a cranky cult which believes he was the Messiah and worships him? It is still innocent, but because of what some people may believe about it, it can become a means of stumbling to them and others. Again, if one has Americans to stay, out of respect for them, we might feel it right to hide it away, since *for them* it is a symbol of oppression and a reminder of the War of Independence. So it is what people believe and understand about things which is the determining factor, not the thing itself. There is no absolute sanctity about things, places or times.

As we look at this priciple we are arriving at the nub of Paul's arguments in Romans 14. So let's pause for a moment and reflect on what really lay behind these statements.

The Heart of the Matter

No one knows for sure exactly what the issues at stake were in the church of Rome. It is unlikely that Paul was writing about a Jewish Christian group who were insisting on keeping the law of Moses and its edicts concerning food and festival days. Probably Paul was having to deal with Gentiles who had

Neither Slave Nor Free

conscientious scruples about food and were vegetarian on principle—which, of course, the Jews were not. But it is important for us to grasp the principles, which we can then apply to our quite different situations.

Paul is writing to two sets of people, the strong and the weak (15:1). The strong are those, probably the majority, who feel themselves free from all these taboos about food and so on. The weak, probably a minority, are very strict about these things and are scandalized by the others. Paul quite obviously agrees with the strong. That is where he stands. He is not in bondage to anything, even to freedom itself! He is prepared, after giving thanks over it, to eat anything within reason. But he is not going to give an absolute ruling on this. Both sides are to tolerate each other. Paul is not going to take sides.

What is interesting is that most of his injunctions are directed at the *weak* rather than the strong. They are the ones who are being stroppy. They are the intolerant and judgmental people. They are the people who are condemning the "free" ones. They are guilty of intimidation. Actually most of the trouble in our churches is caused by the few die-hards who are weak in moral and numerical strength, but compensate for that by their intransigence and intolerant behavior. They are the ones who judge and despise those who disagree with them. They are usually the ones who are ready to pick a quarrel with anyone.

Paul urges the strong to be tolerant and welcoming of these people, even though he himself disagrees with

THAT WE MAY BE ONE

them, but they are not to get entangled in "disputes over opinions" (14:1).

Now we need to get back to Paul's principle.

5) *We are not to be intimidated by the condemnation of others* (v. 16)

Do not let your good be spoken of as evil

We are not to allow our scruples and our convictions on controversial issues to become a slanging match between God's people. There are some people who complain of being "persecuted" when they would have been wiser to have kept their mouth shut. We are neither to intimidate those with whom we disagree nor be intimidated ourselves by the contrary opinions of others. We are neither to express nor give way to aggressive speech. Often we shall find that the time taken up with heated discussions and arguments could have been better employed in more fruitful and edifying conversation. Paul says the same thing a little later. We must always be careful of self-deception when we imagine we are striving for God's truth, whereas in fact we are boosting our own egos or getting our own back on those who have hurt us in the past. Christians sometimes have longer memories than anyone else.

6) *We are to distinguish between essentials and non-essentials* (v. 17)

For the Kingdom of God is not food and drink but righteousness and peace and joy in the Holy Spirit

Neither Slave Nor Free

Here we run into immediate difficulties which we need to be frank about. As we have already seen, not all Christians are agreed as to what constitutes "essentials" and "non-essentials." It is fairly easy to see that vegetarianism, which was the controversial issue in Rome, is something that most Christians, at least today, would place in the non-essential category. But some of the issues I have raised would be regarded by some as "essential" and others as "non-essential." For instance, water baptism would be regarded by most Christians as "essential," but some Christians would regard "believers' baptism" as "essential," whereas others, like myself, would not. I believe water baptism is "essential" (not for salvation but for correct apostolic order in the Church), but the mode of baptism (immersion, pouring, etc.) and the subjects of baptism (children or adults) are issues about which Christians may have different opinions, and the proper ordering of the Church is not affected by these differences. In that sense I would call these differences "non-essential." But I know that there are some from the Baptist-type tradition who would beg to differ and regard their own view as "essential."

It is quite impossible to resolve this area of controversy which has been long with us, and the only alternative to separating ourselves from one another is to agree to differ and to allow each other that right to have these convictions, and let the arguments continue but not to get them out of proportion. A great deal of Christian unity, evangelism, revival, renewal and deep

THAT WE MAY BE ONE

Christian fellowship has taken place between those on either side of this divide. God's blessing does not seem to be conditional on one view or the other.

But leaving aside this kind of problem, there are other differences which are more easily distinguishable as "essential" or "non-essential." The important thing to notice here is that "righteousness and peace and joy in the Holy Spirit" are essential and taboos about "food and drink" are non-essential, and we must seek to apply this same principle wherever possible.

7) *We should concentrate on what builds up and makes peace (v. 19)*

> *Let us then pursue what makes for peace and for mutual upbuilding*

Unfortunately there are some people who love quarrels and take every opportunity in indulging themselves in them. They have an effective armory of weapons which are well sharpened and ready for use. They have become adept through practice at all the artifices of argument and to them it is a game which they are ready to play with anyone. Alas, as far as Christians are concerned, it is a game which neither side generally wins and, in the end, there is more evidence of the flow of adrenalin than of truth. There is a place for argument and controversy amongst Christians, provided our ultimate objective and the underlying principle behind what we are doing is the pursuit of peace and building each other up, rather

Neither Slave Nor Free

than to be warring with each other in order to crush our opponents with the sheer weight of our arguments.

Paul makes it clear that there are two tragic possibilities if we don't pursue a correct course in this respect. We can actually destroy the work of God (v. 20), and cause our fellow Christians to stumble and fall (v. 21). What a tragedy when a great work of God is destroyed because Christians can't stop arguing about non-essentials! The sad fact is that this has happened repeatedly. Christians get the whole thing out of proportion. Satan gets in on the act. Christians turn their attention to one another rather than unitedly wrestling against satanic forces. The people of God are divided against themselves. Civil war breaks out. It is amazing how controversies over comparatively trivial matters can destroy God's work and seriously harm the spiritual lives of Christians, quite apart from the influence this has on those who are not yet Christians, who are seriously offended when they hear and see Christians bickering. How unattractive and inhospitable the Church appears!

8) *We are not to flaunt our faith in front of others* (v. 22)

> *Don't flaunt your faith in front of others who might be hurt by it*

One could almost substitute the word "convictions" for "faith" in this verse. It would seem that both sides in this controversy in Rome may have been claiming that they were the faithful ones in contrast to the others. They felt it necessary to make much of their "faith," showing it off to their opponents. Paul is saying that this is wrong because the object of "faith" is God not our fellow believers. If we have faith, then it has to do with our relationship with God and should never be used as a stick with which to beat our opponents. There are few things less becoming to a Christian than to enter into a kind of "faith competition" with other Christians—"everything you can believe in, I can believe in more."

9) *We are to be patient with the failings of others* (15:1)

> *We who are strong ought to bear with the failings of the weak, and not to please ourselves*

Here is a special message for strong Christians, or those who think they are strong: be patient with the weak, or those you think are weak. Who are these "strong" and "weak" Christians? Appearances can be so deceptive. Sometimes we can put on a show of strength to cover up our weakness. Small dogs bark louder than the big ones. Sometimes a weak front can be a cover for a strong interior. But Paul makes clear that there should always be a home in the Church for weak Christians, and others who are stronger need to be patient with them. They may not be able to keep up with the rest of the Church, but that does not mean

Neither Slave Nor Free

they should be left behind in the race for our high calling in Christ.

10) *We are to welcome one another* (v. 7)

Welcome one another as Christ has welcomed you

This whole passage begins and ends with a welcome. The strong are to welcome the weak (14:1), and the weak the strong (15:7). It may be that Paul has changed the direction of his argument here to the Jewish-Gentile divide, but the principle is the same. Jesus Christ welcomes all who come to Him. In the days of His flesh, He welcomed both Jews and Gentiles. He had amongst His apostolic band the strong and weak. So, too, we should welcome one another in Christ, even if we do disagree with one another. In fact, we should do it even more when we are in disagreement. Paul goes on to draw the attention of the Roman Christians to Christ's servant role. He was a servant to the circumcised (v. 8). That is the role we should adopt towards one another, as servants not as gladiators bent on beating each other to the ground. When we have the servant mentality, then we shall do no harm to one another, and the inevitable differences that we have will be resolved in the right spirit.

8
Tension Points

We all know, and are occasionally made painfully aware of, tension points when our differences surface and when sometimes, alas, conflict breaks out between Christians holding opposite viewpoints. We should not bend over backwards to please everyone and pretend that the difficulties do not exist, or are exaggerated (when they are not) or, if they do exist, that they are two perfectly good ways of saying the same thing. But neither do we want to pursue controversy for its own sake. If there is a legitimate way of resolving differences, let us seek it, provided our personal integrity is not compromised.

I want to deal with five tension points, all of which relate to our broader subject of how renewal can take place without dividing the Church. They are issues which today are causing tension between Christians and are potentially divisive. Here they are:

1. *Water baptism:* does God accept infant baptism or should believers' baptism by immersion be the rule in the church?

THAT WE MAY BE ONE

2. *Scripture and traditions:* how far should we permit in the Church traditions which, though not necessarily contrary to scripture, are not found in it?

3. *The ministry of women:* what role should women play in the Church and, may they be leaders?

4. *The ministry of apostles and prophets:* should we be looking for such ministries in the Church today?

5. *The Second Coming:* is Jesus Christ returning soon, and if He is, how should this affect the way in which we view the Church and its structures?

Now these are all hot issues at the present time, particularly between those who are involved in renewal within the historic churches and others who either believe this to be impossible or feel they have a mandate from God to start new churches. Here are some of the tension points between the "stay-inners" and the "come-outers." Actually this kind of tension has occurred many times before in the history of the Church, though the tension points have sometimes been different. We should also add that these tension points are to be found in other areas of the Church than the Charismatic Renewal.

In this book I shall not attempt to do justice to these five areas of disagreement. To try to do so would mean writing a very much larger book, or even a library of books. Naturally I have my own convictions about each of them, and I do not want to disguise this fact. However, I have friends on both sides of the fence, and

Tension Points

even if one cannot at this stage, as one would like, take the fence down, I hope I can convince the reader that I have a healthy respect for those I disagree with and want to continue to keep my ears open to hearing what they have to say. Nevertheless, these are all serious issues which we need to face together. It does not help if we enter into a mud-slinging competition, or suggest that our friends are either foolish or blind to hold a contrary position to our own. Jesus warned us about the dangers of saying to anyone, "You fool."

In the famous section of the book of Revelation which is normally called "the letters to the Seven Churches," the first one is addressed to the church in Ephesus. While the Lord commends them for the action they have taken against false apostles and teachers, He nevertheless has this against them: they have abandoned the love they had at first (Rev. 2:1 ff). In Milligan's Commentary on this passage he suggests, as William Barclay does also, that there is a connection between the two—that in their zeal to deal with the heretics they had abandoned the love that characterized their church life at the start. In place of that love, in other words, there had come a harsh judgmental spirit. Milligan writes about the place of love in this context, "it is true love which teaches us to win and not to alienate, to raise and not to crush, those who may only be mistaken in their views and are not determined enemies of God." We are not, in sharing about these tension points, dealing with those who are "the enemies of God," but a number of humanly weak

THAT WE MAY BE ONE

Christians who are prone to errors and mistakes which can easily blur the truth. It is always sad to see Christians becoming dogmatic and condemnatory of those with whom they disagree on issues about which there has seldom been a common mind in the Church. Such postures only alienate God's people from one another and mar the united witness and testimony of the Church.

The Underlying Differences

In some ways, we need to take some steps back and look behind the tension points to try to perceive if there may not be differences which in certain ways affect our examination of all these particular issues. There are, I believe, two of these which I want to call "the underlying differences." Here we come face-to-face with major problems of different approaches which, as they stand at present, cannot be easily reconciled. These differences have radically affected controversy between Christians for hundreds of years.

1) *Doctrine of the Church*

Throughout this book I have referred blandly to "the Church." I realize that those who read this book will understand different things from the use of that word. Some will think of their particular denomination, others of their own local congregation, while others still will think of the whole company of born-again and committed Christians, whatever denomination or local

Tension Points

church they may belong to. There are other views which would differ from these I have mentioned, and generally speaking there is still much confusion and misunderstanding on this subject.

However, in this introduction to the tension points I believe I need to clarify where the major fault lines exist between, broadly speaking, two main understandings about the Church.

For some hundreds of years, there have been Christians who have held strongly to the belief that "the Church" consists of all truly committed believers. It has sometimes been called "the gathered Church." Christians are to be separate from the rest of society, to be an "alternative society." Membership of the Church, which in one sense is only known to God, consists of those who have been truly born again, made a profession of faith and been baptized as believers by total immersion in water. With some variations in viewpoint, this position would be taken by the Baptists, Mennonites, Plymouth Brethren, Quakers (or Society of Friends), Congregationalists, Pentecostals and House Churches. In the past they have often come into radical confrontation with State churches and were at times ruthlessly and unchristianly persecuted by the establishment. These people have had a vision of a pure, united Church of completely dedicated Christians. The major problem, of course, has been that such churches, for various reasons, do not remain "pure" and "dedicated." However skillfully men guard against it, the lofty ideals

THAT WE MAY BE ONE

of the founders become tarnished in time. Is there an inevitability about it? Whether there is or there isn't, the track of church history is unfortunately littered with the wreckage of those who have set out in good heart with the finest possible aspirations, but their failure somewhere along that pathway has meant that yet another church which sprang up to try again to find the perfect combination has failed to make it.

The other main view of the Church is that it has always been and always will be a mixed gathering of people, and that it is not for us to judge those who are the Lord's anyway (2 Tim. 2:19). Thus entry to the Church is through the gateway of baptism, often administered to babies fairly soon after they have been born. Such churches have a wide variety of viewpoints. The Roman Catholic church, the Presbyterians and the Methodists are this type of Church. They are larger than the other churches and have within their ranks large numbers of nominal believers whose commitment to Christ and the Church is often quite small. They are often encumbered with unwieldly structures, which if they are tightly controlled and, therefore, inflexible, make renewal extremely difficult. Most of these churches have a long history of renewal movements which they have often been able to contain within their ample borders. Sometimes there has been schism, in fact one of them (the Methodist church) was a renewal movement within the Anglican church which, due to Anglican inflexibility, broke away from that church in the eighteenth century. The major

Tension Points

problem with this kind of church viewpoint is that renewal movements have a much tougher time of it. But in some senses it is a question of timing. The problems which immediately become apparent when a new movement starts in one of the historic churches, will also surface years later in the new churches which start off with such energy and success.

At this stage, I am not going to evaluate further these two basic views of the Church. I am only mentioning them now because they do influence the view that people have of the tension points I'm going to deal with later in this book. An obvious example is the matter of water baptism. Those who believe the Church should only consist of "true believers" will adopt a view of water baptism which conforms to it, namely, believers' baptism by immersion. Similarly, those who have a much more comprehensive view of the Church will accept a much broader concept of baptism, and, therefore, be able to accept infant baptism as one of the appropriate ways of baptizing people.

It is just possible to believe that these two viewpoints, which are so unmistakably different from each other, can be seen as complementary. Could not those who hold these different positions come to accept each other as genuine expressions of "Church?" Is it not possible to see the gathered concept of the Church as an extension of the comprehensive concept, rather as the Catholic church in the past came to accept the religious orders

THAT WE MAY BE ONE

as a special and important extension of its own life? Both concepts are "Church." Perhaps we can accept them both.

2) *The doctrine of Scripture*

Here we must face the other underlying difference, which is rather more serious and affects our understanding of the Church as well as many other areas where Christians are in contention with each other. Broadly speaking, there are three main viewpoints which Christians hold with reference to Scripture and how it should influence our lives, the decisions we make and the practices we follow in our life together in the Church.

1. The first viewpoint would be those who do not accept the supreme authority of Scripture. We may call this the liberal interpretation. There are many variations of this viewpoint, from those who affirm much of Scripture to those who deny most of it.

2. The second viewpoint is that of those who, while accepting the supreme authority of Scripture, are prepared to accept in some instances that which, although not actually contained in the Scriptures, is not contrary to them. An example of this would be infant baptism, the use of liturgies, and the keeping of Easter, Christmas and other church festivals. Actually, to be more precise, there are possible references in the Scriptures to infant baptism, and in a number of other passages there are the germs of liturgical structure,

Tension Points

and the keeping of special days is nowhere prohibited in the New Testament, while the Old Testament has many references to them. Those who take this viewpoint would also want to distinguish in the New Testament between what is mandatory, that is clearly commanded by our Lord and revealed as God's will for His people for all time, and those things which were meant only for the generation to which the writings were originally addressed. Also, they would want to make a distinction between those statements in the New Testament which are dependent on cultural practices which, though generally relevant in the first century, are not necessarily of application to our own. For example, was the place of women, and the way in which the New Testament dealt with the matter, dependent in some way upon the social standing of women in the first century and, therefore, not to be applied to our own situation in the twentieth century, which is obviously very different? The question of women wearing veils when they pray is another example of this, since it was a first-century practice which no longer pertains in western society. We shall have to look carefully at this when we come to examine the third tension: the ministry of women in the Church today.

This viewpoint does not believe that the New Testament is a blueprint for Church order, especially in the area of our understanding of the Church and its ministry. It notes variety in the New Testament itself and this would indicate that even in the first century

THAT WE MAY BE ONE

there was no recognized blueprint for ministries in the Church.

3. The third viewpoint says that we should believe nothing and do nothing unless it is clearly indicated in the New Testament. The Scriptures contain all that we need not only for salvation (which the Church of England also affirms in the Thirty-Nine Articles), but for all matters of church order and ethics. For example, since apostles and prophets are clearly designated in the New Testament as an important and indeed primary ministry, therefore we must have apostles and prophets today, and, in their view, we shall be disobedient if we settle for anything less. The same viewpoint would reject episcopal ministries on the grounds that they belong to a later development after the New Testament had been written, and, although the word is mentioned in the New Testament, it is only an alternative for the word "elder" and, therefore, there is no justification for the office of bishop as it has been understood in the Church from the second century onwards.

I have tried to set the stage for our consideration of the tension points, so let's now turn to the first one—water baptism.

9

Water Baptism, Infants or Adults?

Water baptism is practiced almost universally throughout the Christian Church; but the way in which it is administered and the people who are baptized vary from church to church. There is a growing unity amongst Christians in two areas. In the first place, most churches acknowledge that baptism in and of itself does not confer salvation on the recipient. Most people now reject any mechanical concept of baptismal grace which seems, in effect, to make baptism the savior rather than Christ. In the case of infant baptism, it is now increasingly agreed that the persons baptized have later to confirm and make their own the promises made on their behalf at that baptism. Opinions vary regarding what baptism actually is or does. For Roman Catholics and Anglicans, although there are differences of viewpoint between and within these churches, the general view is that baptism is not a mere sign. To use the language of the Reformers, it is an "effectual sign." Baptismal grace is not only promised in baptism, it is actually conferred in some way through the sacrament. At this point, some Christians would disagree, believing baptism to be only a sign, although it is interesting that a growing number of house church teachers seem to be taking a new line in seeing baptism as something more than just a sign.

The second area of common agreement is that re-baptism is wrong in the sight of God, a rejection of God's offer of His grace which is made in baptism. There are still a few Baptists (particularly the Southern Baptists in the United States) who re-baptize some of their new members who have formerly been members of other Baptist churches, even when they have been baptized already as believers by total immersion; but this is comparatively rare. However, we need to recognize immediately that this large measure of agreement disguises a serious area of disagreement. Those who believe in believers' baptism will invariably re-baptize anyone who was not a "believer" at their first baptism, particularly those who were baptized as children or babies. For them it is not a re-baptism since they believe the first baptism was invalid and unacceptable to God.

At this point, we need to try to understand the two positions and act sensitively, since these points of view are often held tenaciously by both sides and cause grief. For instance, re-baptism as understood by some Roman Catholics and Anglicans is offensive to them. We need, therefore, to move cautiously, respecting this viewpoint even if we do not agree with it. On the other hand, Baptists and others feel deeply about the concept of believers' baptism and have in the past

Water Baptism, Infants or Adults?

centuries been grievously persecuted for their belief. Their views also need to be respected, even if we disagree with them. Caught in the middle of these arguments are those Christians who feel the need for another baptism in water because they believe their first baptism, for various reasons, was inadequate and unacceptable to God. What are they to do about it?

It is these people, of all people, whom we need to help most. I have now met hundreds who have been through what I would call a re-baptism; I have yet to meet one who has asked for it for improper reasons. They are usually keen and committed Christians who see this need for another baptism as a step of obedience to Christ, often a way of expressing some new-found faith and commitment which has meant a great deal to them. The worst thing we can do is to treat them as if they have committed some terrible sin. Above all, we should never question their membership of a particular church. Usually, if they are asking for another baptism, it is to be a better servant of Christ within their own church. I personally think they have mistaken what the Lord is saying to them, *because He was in that first baptism of theirs and recognizes it.* Nevertheless, we need to help and encourage people at this moment, and, although we should make it clear that we don't believe re-baptism (as I would call it) is necessary, yet we do need to love and respect them for their convictions and pray that the Lord will bless them in it.

THAT WE MAY BE ONE

The Depth of Water

I want to return to the theme we started with in a moment, but let me digress for a moment and try to clear up the question of whether baptism should be by immersion, pouring, or sprinkling. Contrary to some mistaken ideas, the Church of England has always stood for baptism by immersion or dipping, only permitting affusion when the child to be baptized is too weak physically for immersion. The Church of England has never permitted sprinkling, though it is often accused by people of doing so. But the Church of England has in this area, as well as others, been inconsistent in its practice. Having inherited thousands of stone fonts which make immersion difficult for children and impossible for adults, it has *in practice* baptized the majority of its people by pouring water on to their heads rather than immersing them. The new Alternative-Service Book, which was authorized in 1980 and complements the old Prayer Book of 1662, continues with the same practice. The priest is told to dip the child in the water or to pour water on him. The same is prescribed for adult baptism, which incidentally now comes *before,* not after, the baptism of infants (as in the old Prayer Book), an indication that the Church of England is now awake to the fact that it ministers in a largely pagan society in which increasingly adult baptism will be the norm rather than infant baptism. It may also be said that it is more accurate now to refer to this as "believers' baptism" rather than "adult baptism," since the term "adult

Water Baptism, Infants or Adults?

baptism" is not used and the call is clear throughout the service that it is for those who definitely believe in the Lord Jesus Christ and are prepared publicly to affirm their allegiance to Christ. The words are explicit: "You must with your own mouth and from your own heart declare your allegiance to Christ . . ." Of course, one cannot guarantee the people mean what they say; but neither can Baptists.

But to get back to the matter of the depth of water, the word "to baptize" in the Greek language means "to dip" and that normally means "to immerse." It would seem from what we know of the early practice of the Church, that immersion was the normal way of administering baptism and is still practiced by the Eastern Orthodox church, even when babies are baptized. But it would also seem from what we know of New Testament practice, that it was never a matter of obligation, nor were those who had not been immersed adjudged to have been improperly baptized. On the Day of Pentecost, for example, over three thousand were baptized in Jerusalem in one day, and it is inconceivable either that they all went down to the Jordan to be baptized or that they were all immersed in the city's limited water supplies. I think we have a distorted view of God if we really believe that He is a stickler when it comes to the depth of water and whether people really do go right under. But that the proper way to baptize people is by immersion would seem beyond contradiction. If this is so, then we should, so far as is possible, baptize people by immersion, whether infants or adults. This means we should dispense with using small fonts, build a proper baptistry, if this is possible, or use at the appropriate time a local river, when the baptism really can be public as it was always meant to be. A friend of mine now sometimes uses the Thames (mercifully freer from pollution than it has been for hundreds of years) and another brought in a child's paddling pool to baptize a young Jewish man in full view of his Jewish parents, who were most impressed. If only the Church of England had, through these centuries, followed the rules faithfully, there would be fewer problems of tension with other Christians—although, perhaps, more with the non-Christian world around us. I would hazard a guess, too, that there would be fewer nominal Christians. Baptism often means more to people when they are totally immersed and it speaks more clearly about our total response to the challenge of Christian discipleship as well as the depth of God's love and Christ's salvation into which we truly are "immersed" when we are joined to Him.

Are Children Eligible for Baptism?

We need to return now to the main point of contention and where there is more definite disagreement. The main argument advanced by those who reject infant baptism is that baptism is for "believers" and, therefore, it is only appropriate when a person is able to make a personal response of faith to the grace of God. The authority for this is drawn from the New

Water Baptism, Infants or Adults?

Testament, particularly statements like, "He who believes and is baptized will be saved . . ." (Mark 16:16) and, "Go and make disciples of all nations, baptizing them in the name of the Father and of the Son and of the Holy Spirit, teaching them to observe all that I have commanded you . . ." (Matt. 28:19-20). Since baptism here, so the argument goes, is for those who believe and those who are disciples, it cannot refer to babies or those who, as yet, are unable to make a real response to the gospel of Christ.

Interpreting Scripture

I am not going to work exhaustively through all the arguments for and against child baptism—a field which has been ploughed many times before and by far more skillful hands than my own. But the problem needs to be pointed out at this stage, although the answer is difficult to find. Earlier I stressed that Christians interpret the Bible in different ways, and this constitutes a major part of the problem. Some would argue (as from the two texts already mentioned) that nowhere in the New Testament is there explicit reference to infant or child baptism and, therefore, we must presume, because of the absence of clear evidence to the contrary, that believers' baptism is mandatory. Other argue that, although this is true, nowhere in the New Testament is there any explicit prohibition of infant baptism, and there are a few inferences that it was practiced in the early Church (e.g. the baptism of the Philippian jailer *and his*

THAT WE MAY BE ONE

household, and the reference by Paul in 1 Corinthians 7:14 to children being holy because of the faith of at least one of the parents). There is also the parallel between circumcision, which was administered to male children in infancy and baptism, although in my opinion this is not a very strong argument.

Certainly it can be argued (on the basis of the Old and New Testament concept of the Covenant) that infant baptism is not inconsistent with biblical teaching. But the main point I am making is that our differences do depend also on how we interpret the Scriptures and how we relate them to church life. One side believes Scripture is clear and mandatory, the other that it is not. What we need to avoid at all costs is swearing at one another! The theological swear words in this context are "fundamentalist" and "liberal" or "compromiser." We are not to accuse one another of disobeying God when it is not clear to some Christians that obedience is really at stake.

Understanding Children

One important way of approaching this controversial issue is in the development of an understanding of how God himself looks upon children. It is well known that those who lived at the same time as Jesus and were the main teachers in His day had a very low opinion of children, some actually arguing that they did not have souls, but that the soul entered their bodies at a later date! Jesus went out of His way to receive and bless children. In Matthew 18, sometimes called "the

Water Baptism, Infants or Adults?

children's charter," Jesus calls a child (the word used is a diminutive, "little child") to Him and challenges His audience to "become like children" to enter the Kingdom of Heaven. Jesus also makes it clear that children can believe in Him. He actually refers to those who "believe in me" and tells the crowd that they are to "receive" them in His name and in doing so, they will be receiving Christ. When children were later brought to Him for blessing (Matt. 19:13-15), the disciples tried to prevent the parents and actually rebuked them for doing so. Jesus, however, told the disciples they were to let them come, "for to such belongs the Kingdom of Heaven." By this He meant that they were already in the Kingdom.

These passages have sometimes been used as an argument for infant baptism. Directly—they are not, since blessing not baptism is in view, and in any case Jesus did not baptize people, even adults. But indirectly it speaks powerfully to us because it reveals Jesus' attitude to children and how highly He regarded them.

Let me put it this way. Most churches which do not practice infant baptism do have a service of dedication and blessing for newly born children. They are offered in faith to God. The question I want to ask is: what does God do in response to that offer? There is only one answer: "He receives them." If He receives them, and according to Jesus they are already in the Kingdom, "what hindereth them from being baptized?" My answer would be, "nothing."

THAT WE MAY BE ONE

It is surely not inappropriate to ask again the question: why, if the Holy Spirit knew ahead of time that such controversies would arise, did He not settle these issues once and for all? It would only have needed one sentence or two: "Though shalt not baptize infants" or "Thou shalt only baptize those who can make a meaningful response to God in faith." That would have settled it for all time. Surely we should not be dogmatic on issues in which Scripture itself is not dogmatic. On this Christians have been divided for centuries, so it ill befits us to lay down the law to one another.

In recent years, medical knowledge has increased rapidly and psychological studies have developed almost from scratch so that we have a much greater understanding of human growth from conception to birth and from birth to puberty.

Everything seems to point to human consciousness and perception developing much earlier than it was previously supposed. Yes, children do have souls, and the origins of consciousness have to be traced back to before birth. The human fetus has been shown to be responsive months before birth takes place and one of the strong arguments against the free practice of abortion is that hurt and suffering does occur in the human fetus and psychological studies show that sicknesses of the mind may originate in the womb. Doctors also stress the need for healthy mental attitudes in the mother before as well as after birth, since fetuses do respond favorably or adversely to

Water Baptism, Infants or Adults?

many stimuli, especially, as one would expect, from the pregnant mother. If John the Baptist could be filled with the Holy Spirit from his mother's womb, so can anyone else, and so it is surely possible for babies to become regenerate even before they are able to respond mentally and express their faith in words of public confession. It is unthinkable that a person's salvation depends on his ability to speak, understand and respond to the gospel of Christ, otherwise it would rule out the mentally retarded or abnormal.

In the end, much depends on where you want to put the stress in baptism. Is it, as some see it, chiefly the human response to the divine initiative, a way of expressing our decision to follow Jesus Christ? Or is it, as others see it, chiefly the sign of the divine initiative and that salvation is God's gift, not a result of our decision to follow Christ? Personally I believe the latter is the more scriptural and healthy emphasis. The docility of the baby is a splendid reminder to all who witness the baptism of an infant that we can do nothing either to deserve or obtain our salvation, which is all of God. All we can do, whether we are children or adults, is to rest in the arms of Jesus and receive His love and grace.

Responsible Baptism

I am personally convinced that my own baptism as an infant at a Church of England font has been accepted by God, and the later commitment of my life to Christ does not necessitate my being (as I would

THAT WE MAY BE ONE

call it) re-baptized. But having said that, the Church does need to preserve the sacred rite of baptism from abuse, and my own church has not always done that. I cannot see how one can justify the indiscriminate granting of baptism to the children of parents who are quite definitely not committed disciples of Christ. The only way in which infant baptism can possibly be justified is when it is administered to the children of families in which at least one of the parents is a committed Christian. Here the difficulty may be in determining who is "a committed Christian," and we may well have to give the benefit of the doubt to some whose faith may not seem to be valid. But we must never forget the child itself, for the baptism is primarily for the benefit of him, and, most important of all, the Lord Jesus Christ, who never refused children when they were brought to Him—nor questioned the parents as to the state of their spiritual health.

I hope this will be some help to those who are perplexed by this tension point. However strongly we may feel about this issue, we should never allow it to separate ourselves from one another. Our unity is in Jesus Christ and the Holy Spirit, not in when or how we happened to have been baptized, or even whether we have been baptized at all.

A Theological Note

For those who want to explore this subject further, I would recommend the Lima Text on "Baptism, Eucharist and Ministry." This was produced by the

Water Baptism, Infants or Adults?

Faith and Order Commission of the W.C.C. and published in 1982. The Roman Catholic church, though not a member of the W.C.C., is an active participant in the Faith and Order Commission. The Lima Text represents the most significant convergence on views on baptism that has yet been known. Many of the views that I have expressed in this chapter are also the views of this report: the necessity of faith to receive salvation, the need for the public confession of faith (in the case of infants at a later date), the need for pastoral nurturing, the inappropriateness of both re-baptism and indiscriminate baptism, and the value of immersion.

10

Traditions, Human or Divine?

We are all of us creatures of habit and followers of tradition. Every morning, I read from the same version of the Bible and pray in the same room. I sit at the same chair for breakfast and eat the same kind of cereal. I read the same newspaper and open the mail in the same way. I am probably more traditional than most, but our whole life, for most of the time, is affected if not dominated by habit and traditions.

When we transfer this to the Church sphere, some reach for their weapons. We are all too ready either to defend our traditions or to attack the traditions of others, or even to think that we don't have any and are free from their influence. No one is more traditional than a person who is trying not to be traditional.

Let's first try to answer the question: "What is tradition?" Unfortunately, it has too often been treated disdainfully by those who, thinking they are echoing the sentiments of Jesus Christ, believe it is their duty to reject all traditions of men in favor of the word and will of God. The word "tradition" itself, however, is perfectly innocent and neutral. It simply means the process whereby beliefs or customs are handed down

THAT WE MAY BE ONE

from one generation to another. It is used in this sense by Paul in 2 Thessalonians 2:15, "stand firm and hold to the traditions which you were taught by us, either by word of mouth or by letter." In 2 Thessalonians 3:6, the readers are urged to avoid those who are idle and not living "in accord with the tradition that you received from us." Here we must assume that Paul had in mind certain concrete teachings and was not wanting this particular church to pass on every word that he had written and said.

The Christian attitude to tradition can be found beautifully summarized in the fifth commandment: "honor your father and your mother." Tradition, rightly understood, is that which has been handed down to us by our spiritual forefathers. They should be honored and respected, not despised and rejected. To imagine for one moment that every new generation can start again as if all previous generations are neither to be trusted nor listened to, is both arrogant and foolish. But to honor and respect our parents does not mean we have to obey them in everything they say to us. We are to listen respectfully and carefully to all Christian traditions, but we are only bound in the final analysis by our obedience to God himself.

In the early centuries of the Church, the word "tradition" was in fact related closely to God's revelation to the early apostles and prophets. In that sense, both the Old and New Testaments are "tradition" in their entirety. In 2 Timothy 2:2 we have the same principle asserted, "and what you have heard

Traditions, Human or Divine?

from me before many witnesses entrust to faithful men who will be able to teach others also." From the third century, the "tradition" was sometimes expressly identified with the gospel in the Scriptures. Whenever unwritten tradition was mentioned, it was never seen as independent of Scripture, but as customs and teachings which were both consistent with it and confirming of it. However, later "tradition" became detached from Scripture. At its best, it can be seen and surely accepted (though *never* if it is contrary to Scripture) as a bank of the accumulated wisdom and inspiration of the past, the most important part of which would be the way in which Christians have understood the Scriptures; at its worst, it has come into conflict with Scripture itself and been given by some a place in which it judges Scripture rather than is judged by it.

The controversial aspect of all this is *what* is passed on, rather than the actual process whereby it is passed on. Jesus, for example, was not in contention with tradition as such, but with what He called "the tradition of the elders," which in some cases, and Jesus gave concrete examples (Matt. 15:2-6), had actually contradicted and made void the law of God. Equally, Paul contends with what he calls "human tradition" in Colossians 2:8, which was not "according to Christ." Here he was thinking of Greek philosophy which was inconsistent with Christian teaching and ethics.

One of our important tasks is to distinguish between

THAT WE MAY BE ONE

two kinds of tradition. There is the apostolic tradition, which is *written* in the Scriptures. We may have some differences as to how we should receive and interpret this rich legacy to us from the past, but we can be quite clear as to what we are talking about. The other kind of tradition is much more difficult to assess and there can be considerable disagreements amongst Christians. The use of Sunday is an example of a well-established tradition which is almost universally accepted by Christians (the Seventh Day Adventists are an exception), but which is not commanded in the Scriptures. It is a *church* rather than an *apostolic* tradition and plays an important part in the life of the universal Church. We shall be dealing with other church traditions which are more controversial later.

In turning to this tension point, we become immediately aware of the problem we have already raised with water baptism: the differences that exist between some Christians who say they will only believe what is contained in Scripture, and others who say they will believe nothing that is contrary to Scripture.

The celebrating of Christmas, for example, is not a festival laid down in the New Testament. The New Testament, we have already said, has provided us with no book of Leviticus to guide us. But, equally, to celebrate Christmas is not contrary to Scripture. There is no command in the Old or New Testaments which would prohibit it. Here is our difficulty. It would be a natural development from Judaism that the

Traditions, Human or Divine?

Christian Church should have its own festivals. We must not forget that much that was "Christian" was derived from Judaism. The Christian festivals, then, are a logical development. But they can never be made obligatory for Christians since, unlike the Old Testament festivals, they are not commanded, Christians must, therefore, be free to keep festivals like Christmas and Easter should they wish to, or refrain from doing so if that is their wish, and those who take opposite viewpoints should not condemn each other.

Disputes About Traditions in the New Testament

There is a wealth of material in the New Testament on this whole subject and an interesting harmony of views between the teachings of Jesus Christ in the gospels and those of Paul in his letters. It was obviously an important matter for the early Christians to handle situations in which equally devout and committed Christians held opposing views. There are three passages in Paul's letters in which this matter is dealt with in depth. In 1 Corinthians 8, he handles the controversy over "food offered to idols." Apparently in those days, meat and other food was offered to idols before it was sold. Some Christians, therefore, felt it had been desecrated and so could not be bought or eaten. Others disagreed with this viewpoint. In Colossians 2:8-19 he discusses similar matters and asks the Christians not to judge one another "in questions of food and drink or with regard to a festival

THAT WE MAY BE ONE

or a new moon or a sabbath." They are not the reality, Paul writes, but only a shadow. The reality is Christ.

Paul was a man who enjoyed his Christian liberty to the full. He was a free man in Christ, liberated from unchristian inhibitions and taboos. So free was he from all forms of spiritual bondage that he was not even in bondage to his freedom! As he says, *"there is neither slave nor free"* in Christ (Gal. 3:28). Paul was as ready to conform to a Jewish life-style when in their society as he cheerfully accommodated himself to Gentile life-style when with them. The interests of the gospel, the glory of God and the spiritual well-being of people were of much greater interest and concern to him, and to these everything else had to bow.

Paul, however, was a spiritual enough man not to allow his freedom in Christ to condemn those who were not experiencing the same freedom. "Though I am free from all men," he wrote to the Corinthians, "I have made myself a slave to all, that I might win the more" (1 Cor. 9:19). Though naturally a strong personality, he did not use his strength to crush the weak. "To the weak I became weak," he says, "that I might win the weak. I have become all things to all men, that I might by all means save some" (v. 22). Martin Luther said the same thing in his famous pamphlet, "Of the Liberty of a Christian Man": "a Christian man is a most free Lord of all, subject to none. A Christian man is a most dutiful servant of all, subject to all." There it is in a nutshell. At one and the same time the Christian is

Traditions, Human or Divine?

slave and free. But we must now apply some of these principles to present disputes.

Some Present Disputes

It is a sad fact that it would almost take a library of books to set out all the many matters over which Christians have been in dispute down the centuries. No wonder the New Testament has so much to teach about how to handle disputes! Would to God all of us had read and understood these passages more, and then been able to apply them more precisely to areas of dispute.

In this chapter, we are dealing with the question of "traditions." Although the principles we have outlined can also be applied to other areas of controversy, it is of particular application to this one, for the differences that Paul was writing about are similar to those that have arisen again and again in the life of the Church.

It is strange to reflect on the things that have been in contention in the past. When the Puritans were in controversy with the Church of England in its early days, some of the disputes were over comparatively minor issues, like the use of the sign of the cross in services, particularly baptism. Both sides were surely at fault, the Puritans for taking a legalistic attitude to this and other matters and the rest of the Church for not allowing them to hold to their scruples, which would not have endangered the Church and would have caused much less damage than the schism it ultimately provoked. I can remember how contentious

THAT WE MAY BE ONE

the issue of wearing stoles at ordination was when I was myself ordained. I recall a well-known church dignitary standing at the door of the vestry of the cathedral as we moved in for the ordination service, trying to press stoles on those like myself who had refused to wear them. Such were the issues of the day! We laugh at the way men in the past have argued on issues such as how many angels can dance on the head of a pin. But it is hardly less comical (and sad) that Christians have fallen out over candles on the altar, organs in church, turning to the east for the Creed, processions, carrying the cross, kneeling or sitting for prayer, etc. Much of that kind of controversy is a thing of the past and hardly worth the ink to write about. But there are contemporary issues which threaten to keep us arguing well into the twenty-first century. Here are a few of them.

1) *Styles of Worship*

There are some who are adamant: all services should be "spontaneous" and liturgy is unbiblical. To them, the New Testament provides us with a clear blueprint. They had no prayer books in those days, and what was good enough for them should be good enough for us. Any idea of "liturgy" means formality, boring services, vain repetition and quenching the Holy Spirit. They believe it is good to prepare for worship services, but all prayers should be spontaneous, Holy Communion should be taken "if the Spirit moves us," and there should be complete

Traditions, Human or Divine?

freedom throughout the service for spontaneous contributions "from the floor." The basis for this understanding is the statement in 1 Corinthians 14 about worship in the Corinthian church. Thus every service is a new liturgy, every Sunday is a celebration of Easter and we should be led independently of all other Christians in the kind of service we have and its content. To do anything else is grieving God and a form of resistance to the Holy Spirit. It is to be in bondage to "tradition."

This view of worship, with it particular style, has been a feature of the Free Churches since the Reformation, and some smaller churches before then. Within this tradition there have been different emphases. The Quakers have stressed waiting upon God in silence, waiting for the moving of the Spirit. The Baptists have stressed the preaching of the word of God; the Plymouth Brethren "audience participation," though usually only for the men, since women (so they say) are to keep silent in the church. The Pentecostals' stress is on the manifestations of the Spirit and the gifts given to the whole church for its mutual edification. The modern House churches stress all of these, combining the Plymouth Brethren and Pentecostal dimensions.

The other view of worship is different. In the Roman Catholic, Eastern Orthodox, Anglican, Lutheran, Methodist and Presbyterian traditions, stress has been placed on liturgies drawn from the traditions of the past. There are prayer and service books which are in

THAT WE MAY BE ONE

general use throughout these churches, with services for Holy Communion, corporate worship, baptisms, marriages and funerals and other aspects of the corporate life of the Church. Although a modern trend has been to provide for much more variety, on the whole similar services are being used throughout the world in these different kinds of churches.

One of the mistakes we often make is to exaggerate our differences in order to clarify them and identify ourselves. So we see things as "black and white" rather than different shades of grey. Here is a classic example, I have been now to many Free Churches and find them not nearly as "free" as their advocates claim. In recent years, I have also been to a number of the new House churches and can easily detect the development of their own individual style or liturgy. It is often good, sometimes very good. But the point I am making is that it is an exaggeration to say it is all "spontaneous." Some of it has been (rightly) carefully prepared beforehand. Other parts of the service, which are thought to be "spontaneous," are so similar to what has been said and done a hundred times before that one could almost call them "variations on an original theme." That is not to despise them, only to explain that none of us can break entirely free from liturgy.

On the other hand, the critics of liturgical worship often exaggerate the differences and confuse the issue by talking about "straitjackets" and other emotive phrases. Actually there is considerable variation and

Traditions, Human or Divine?

flexibility, especially since the spate of liturgical reform that has taken place in most churches. There is room in these services for spontaneous utterances, though sadly many churches don't take advantage of this and even prohibit them deliberately. Sometimes there is more flexibility in liturgical churches than in modern house churches. The situation is never quite as black and white as some people suggest.

Nor are we being strictly accurate when we say that New Testament worship was *always* spontaneous. We don't know that the Corinthian church was typical, though some aspects of it probably were. It does not seem to have been a model church in many aspects of its life, why in this one? There are several traces in the New Testament of new liturgy forming and it is inconceivable that the church of these days, cradled as it was in Judaism, would have been entirely non-liturgical. It certainly embraced the Psalms, which would have formed an important part of their form of service, as it still does today in Church liturgies.

In a way, it brings us back to what we mean by tradition. Tradition links us with the past, which can teach us a lot, provided we are open also to the new things that the Holy Spirit may be wanting us to do and say. Tradition must always conform with Scripture. One of the oldest traditional forms of worship is the *Te Deum*. Are we to reject it because it is not from the Scriptures? It certainly is scriptural and nowhere contradicts the Bible. It may have been given spontaneously (like a prophecy), possibly on the eve of

THAT WE MAY BE ONE

Augustine's baptism. I think it can be argued that such a superb statement of truth, which has been sung by Christians for more than a millennium, is a healthy link with the past that we should not reject simply because it is not "spontaneous." To spurn the riches of the past is one thing; to replace them with spontaneous utterances which can sometimes be banal and trivial is a great pity. Those who reject the best liturgical traditions of the past often have to suffer from much that is unworthy and light-weight.

2) *Festivals*

Here is another point of disagreement, which has something to do with the passage in Romans 14. In verse 5 Paul says, "One man esteems one day as better than another, while another man esteems all days alike." Here there seems to have been a difference of opinion about the significance of days, perhaps a reference to those who took the sabbath (Saturday) or the new Christian sabbath (Sunday) seriously as a special day, a kind of first-century Sabbatarianism. Still today Christians can be divided into those who take the Christian festivals seriously and those who don't. There are also the two extremes, those who observe the Church's Year in all its detail—Saints' day, Advent, Lent, etc.—and those who reject all Christian festivals, even Christmas and Easter.

Christmas is not, as some assert, a pagan festival with a few Christian overtones. It was not celebrated for three hundred years after Christ and had particular

Traditions, Human or Divine?

significance then owing to the controversies in the Church over the nature of Christ's person. It served a useful purpose in spot-lighting the deity of Christ when others were denying it. It has acquired some pagan elements, many of which were introduced in the last century, brought over to this country from Germany by Queen Victoria's husband, the Prince Consort. But what is more important to notice is that the festival of Christmas was also introduced as part of the deliberate church policy of imposing Christian festivals on top of pagan ones in order to destroy their influence. December 25th was chosen deliberately to oppose a pagan festival which was fixed on that day and commemorated the birth of the sun. Can one really quarrel about that? The sites of pagan worship were often chosen for church buildings for similar reasons.

The story of Easter, however, is quite different, being the greatest and oldest festival of the Church, and relates directly both to the Jewish festival of the Passover and the actual dates and events of the crucifixion and resurrection of Jesus Christ. It has always held the highest place in both the Eastern and Western Church. The name itself is derived from a pagan festival which the commemoration of the resurrection of Jesus superseded. Apart from the name, the essence of the festival is thoroughly Christian. It is perfectly true that we celebrate these events continuously in our lives and every Sunday is a remembrance of the resurrection. Nevertheless, it does seem right once a year for us to have this special

THAT WE MAY BE ONE

focus on Jesus' death and resurrection, just as at Christmas we focus on His birth. It is a link we have with Christians of all churches everywhere in the world, and a great opportunity for witness and testimony with the widespread coverage which the media gives to it. In Britain, large numbers of people do come to churches at Christmas and Easter who don't otherwise show up at all. This chance for them to hear the word of God should not be missed; many do, in time, find the living Lord Jesus Christ through these occasions.

But surely this is not an issue for Christians to fall out over. The keeping of the festivals is not commanded by the Lord. Both those who "esteem all days alike" and those who don't should not feel under each other's judgment and condemnation. Let the principles of Romans 14 apply to both.

3) *Head covering*

There are some churches today of the independent or house church variety which insist on women having their heads covered when they either pray or prophesy in public. When I first saw this happen, I could hardly believe my eyes. A woman in a small prayer meeting took out a scarf, tied it round her head and then began to pray, removing the scarf after she had finished. Of course, it is all there in 1 Corinthains 11 where Paul discussed the question of the relationship between husbands and wives and the leadership which the husband has in his relationship to his wife. Paul makes

Traditions, Human or Divine?

it clear that women should be veiled when they pray or prophesy, whereas men should not cover their heads. It would seem that the women in the church in Corinth were a source of trouble. Later in 1 Corinthians 14:34 Paul orders them to "keep silence in the churches." We will deal with this Scripture later because it belongs to another context (see pages 119-128). The women were clearly acting in a disorderly fashion.

If we can pause for a moment, it was an incredible thing that this was actually a problem in a Christian church! The role of women in both Jewish and Gentile society at that time was totally subordinate to men. The wearing of a veil was a sign of their submission to their husbands. But the Christian gospel had already so liberated the women in this church that they had not only discarded their veils but were beginning to take a dominant position in the life of the church. They had clearly gone too far. From a position in which they had been totally dominated by men, they had moved in a short time to a position in which they had become the dominators. This was as false a position as the one from which they had been liberated.

But what should we do today? Should we take this passage of Scripture and apply it to our worship services? Should we insist on women wearing hats or scarves when they take part? Some people believe we should, and to refrain from doing so is to be disobedient to God's word. If they feel so strongly about it, according to the Romans 14 principles, others who disagree with them should respect their convictions,

THAT WE MAY BE ONE

and if visiting churches submit to their directions. But equally others, like myself, who do not agree with them should be free to disagree and act quite differently.

Again, the issue turns on how we interpret Scripture. Do we take every passsage literally and apply it to every situation? I think not. Here was a particular situation peculiar to the first century. Here was a custom (the wearing of veils) which was relevant in the first century but which is irrelevant today in our western world. What is important is not the outward details, but the principles underneath this passage which are relevant at all times—particularly the domestic relationship between husbands and wives or men and women. So often when you concentrate on the outward, you lose sight of the much more important principles and you get the whole thing out of proportion. I suspect that the real issue itself is being closely clouded by this side issue, and we shall be going into this in much more detail in the next chapter.

I have selected a few of the less serious areas of disagreement between Christians today. We can see how the principles that Paul gives us in Romans 14-15 may be applied. We should apply these same principles to other areas whenever our relationship to one another in Christ is threatened, in order that we may experience that unity for which Christ both prayed and died.

11
Women, Leaders or Led?

A few years ago, I was invited to speak at a large charismatic conference which had just been influenced by the so-called "discipleship" controversy. During the conference, I was asked to come to the daily prayer and planning meetings at which the leadership met to consider the arrangements for the conference. I shall always remember the sense of shock I received when I looked around a room full of about fifty *men*. I had been involved in organizing many conferences, but it had been for me normal and natural to have women involved in the prayer and planning on an equal footing with men. I gathered afterwards that when the discipleship teaching hit this conference, it was decided there and then to exclude all women from these meetings.

This is not the place for me to explain all aspects of the discipleship teaching. The most controversial part of it undoubtedly has been the exercise of strong authority by some Christians over others. The part that concerns us is the virtual denial to women of any part in leadership. They are to be kept firmly under the control and leadership of men. This has always been the emphatic teaching of the Plymouth Brethren, who tend to take literally the command of Paul "that the women should keep silence in the churches" (1 Cor. 14:34). Thus the role of women in the Church should be docile and subordinate to men.

In this chapter, I'm not going to deal with the equally contentious issue of whether women should be ordained to the priesthood. This is not because I deem the issue of no importance. But I want, within the limits of this book, to handle the wider issue as to whether women should have any role of leadership in the Church at all. Certainly there are those, particularly in the house church movement, who would say they should not: Scripture, so they argue, has settled the matter once and for all. Only men can hold positions of leadership in the Church. They alone can take authority over men (and, of course, women).

The Role of Women in the New Testament

We know a great deal about the views on women of Jesus' contemporaries. Pious rabbis in their prayers repeatedly thanked God that they were men and not women. In the synagogues, women were not only veiled, but physically separated from the men, banished to the gallery or some other adjacent room. No woman would dare speak in public and they were to be in total submission to men. Roman society was governed by similar principles and in Roman law women had virtually no rights.

Into this society came Jesus, the Son of God. As soon as He began His public work, He was quickly

Women, Leaders or Led?

scandalizing society by the way in which He not only welcomed women and ministered freely to them, but allowed them to minister to Him. They (together with the twelve disciples) accompanied Him on His missions. In John 4, we realize how shocked even His disciples were when Jesus conversed with a woman in public with no one else present. It is true that He did not include a woman amongst His apostolic band. But had He done so, it is almost certain that the rest would have left.

In a short time, Jesus inaugurated and inspired a revolution in the relationship between the sexes. He started something which the early Church was to continue, so that women figure prominently in ministry in a way that must have been unique for those times. When one considers that it was not until after the First World War that women in Britain were allowed even to vote, that women have achieved the measure of freedom they now possess only after many years of bitter conflict, and that even today sexual discrimination is comparatively commonplace in the West and almost total in most of the rest of the world, one can begin to see how revolutionary Jesus' attitudes were. Jesus might well have gone much further had that been possible. But to get things into proportion, we should measure the achievements of a comparatively few years against the snail-like pace of change in the following centuries.

In the New Testament, eldership is quite clearly envisaged as male. In the well-known passages that

THAT WE MAY BE ONE

describe the functions and qualifications of elders (1 Tim. 3:1-7, Titus 3:5-9), it is clear that only men are in view. For example the writer says that the elder is to be "the husband of one wife" (1 Tim. 3:2) which is reiterated in Titus 1:6. Female eldership was at that time completely out of the question.

Now here again, we come up against the problem of interpretation. If we are required to keep to the letter of the New Testament, then the matter has been settled for ever more. No woman should ever function as a leader in the Church. But the question we are bound to ask is whether this particular principle is binding on us today, as it clearly was in the first century, and whether this principle was preconditioned by the society in which the first-century Church sought to function. In other words, are these statements mandatory for all time, or only of application to those who lived in the first century?

When we look at the relevant texts we do not find a single mandatory statement which rules out as a matter of principle women as leaders in the Church. We shall look in a moment at what Paul wrote about all this to the Corinthians. It would seem that the assumption that all elders should be male stems from the situation and status of women in the first century, and that when subsequently the position of women was to change, that assumption would no longer apply. In other words, the question of whether women should be leaders in the Church, and, therefore, in certain circumstances have authority over men, was decided

Women, Leaders or Led?

according to the circumstances of that time rather than fixed and unchanging principles. I should make it clear that I am not here writing about the relationship of husband and wife. That is another, though related, matter. The issue we are facing concerns women as leaders in the Church, and this applies to unmarried as well as married women.

One might add here that the Old Testament indicates that God's calling and anointing of leadership was sometimes given to women. If the statement in Proverbs 31:10-31 is anything to go by ("A good wife who can find?"), the role of women in home and society was much freer than anything that pertained in the Jewish society into which Jesus Christ was born. We would be well to observe this much more enlightened view of women, which is in stark contrast to the narrow, bigoted viewpoint of the Scribes and Pharisees of Jesus' day. It could be that, in interpreting the New Testament texts so literally, some are, in fact, enforcing the bias of the Scribes and Pharisees rather than the attempts by Jesus and the apostles to release women from bondage to the law into that freedom in which Paul says "there is neither male nor female."

Jewish prejudice had to have a court for the women in the Temple which was separated from those other parts into which men could go. When Jesus died on the cross, not only the veil of the Temple was torn from top to bottom, but the wall separating men from women, figuratively speaking, came crashing down.

THAT WE MAY BE ONE

The Corinthian Hussies

Much has been made of Paul's statements in 1 Corinthians about women and their role in the Church. We need to remember that Paul was writing to the members of the Church in a city which was notorious for its decadence in an age of unbridled sensuality. The women had been imprisoned by repressive taboos and often treated as sex objects by men; now in Christ they had been released. They were free. They were respected as people with human rights and dignity. It is not surprising under these circumstances that they swung too far in the opposite direction and had begun to use their new freedom to dominate and disturb the peace and unity of the Church.

We need to see Paul's statements in the light of this situation. In 1 Corinthians 14:34 he is *not* prohibiting women from taking part in public worship alongside men. In 11:5 he envisages women both praying and prophesying, and the statement in 1 Timothy 2:12 prohibiting women from teaching in the Church should not necessarily be applied to our situation today. When those words were written, there had not yet been established a norm of any kind for Christian doctrine. No creeds had been universally acknowledged and the New Testament documents had yet to be collected, indeed some had not even been written. Once the norms had been established and accepted there was no reason, other than male prejudice, why women should not teach from the Scriptures, as

Women, Leaders or Led?

indeed many women have done for the benefit of the whole Church.

All sexual domination is sinful, whether it be male or female. Women's Liberation has often been as restricting and harmful to men as the opposite has been to women. Both men and women should lay down their arms, recognize each other's gifts, encourage one another to share them in ministry, and work in harmonious cooperation together. It would be a great mistake to read into Paul's letters to the Corinthians hard and fast rules which must be enforced in every church situation. The Corinthian church was a special case for which we can be very thankful, for we have a great deal of information which we might not otherwise have, if it had been a more normal and stable church. But we would be foolish to build unchanging doctrines on some of Paul's statements to them.

The Situation Today

The situation we face today in the western world is in marked contrast to that of the first century. A hundred years ago, there were very few professions or jobs in which women could find a place, apart from the menial. Florence Nightingale had to fight every inch of the way to open the nursing profession to them. How all that has changed! We now have not only women Members of Parliament, but a woman Prime Minister. Women have directorships of companies, they are judges and barristers, consultants and surgeons,

THAT WE MAY BE ONE

airline pilots and bus drivers. There are few positions which have not at one time or another been filled by women. In all this the Church, which used to be the protector and encourager of women in society, has become the back-marker.

Much of this change has been gain. Thousands of women have found fulfillment they never knew before. Single and divorced women have found a niche in society, and an opportunity to use their gifts which had been denied them for centuries. But it has not been all gain. There has been some serious loss, and it may be with this in mind that some Christians express their reactionary opinions and take their strong stand against female leadership.

Only women can be mothers, and that is to put it at its starkest. But it is not only a physical fact, it is a spiritual fact also. Women have a unique function in relationship not only to child-bearing but the nurturing of children from the moment of conception. We need to add that the father has an equally important role alongside the mother. But it is a different role and obviously cannot take the place of the mother. There is plenty of evidence to show that an increasingly serious social factor is the gradual retreat from these responsibilities, by both mothers and fathers. It is this fact, and the fear that accompanies it, which may in part explain the new insistence by some that a mother's place is in the home and her chief role is the bearing and nurturing of children.

Having said all that, it would seem to me an

Women, Leaders or Led?

inadequate excuse for curbing the role and function of women as leaders in the Church. It leaves out of account, in any case, single women who are not called upon to have children, and married women who may be childless. It should be our concern that mothers accept their full responsibilities with fathers to care adequately for their children and not to neglect them. But as the years pass, mothers do become more free and should be allowed, as time and opportunity permit, the chance to share in the leadership of the Church alongside the men.

What has happened in other professions has shown that some women do possess leadership qualities which can be sanctified and set to use for the blessing of the Church. If one accepts the principle of the plurality of leadership, there need be no fears of a female "take-over." Whether women should be bishops, ministers or chief pastors is another issue, which I have tried to deal with in greater detail in my book, *Let My People Grow*. Leaving that aside, I have tried in this chapter to handle the wider issue of female leadership in partnership with men, and my strong conviction that women can and should be involved in both the policy-forming and decision-making processes in the Church. That, so far as I see it, is part of the elementary human rights that all women have; to deny it can only cause harm to women in general and loss to the Church, which stands to gain immeasurably from their gifts and talents.

12

Apostles and Prophets, True or False?

In recent years, there has been renewed interest in the recognition of the ministry of apostles in the Church. Some of the newly formed house churches have actually appointed or recognized apostles as leaders in their fellowships and this has become another area of tension, which I am proposing now to try to deal with.

A lot obviously depends on whether it was ever intended that apostles should continue as leaders in the Church with the kind of authority that they had in the first century, and so our first step must be to study the New Testament itself.

Apostles in the New Testament

It is obvious from even the simplest study of the New Testament that the word "apostle" is used in a variety of ways. At times the word describes the most exalted of ministries, particularly the Twelve whom Jesus chose to be His companions during His short earthly ministry. But it is also used to describe much humbler work. In 2 Corinthians 8:23 and Philippians 2:25, it is used to describe the work of virtual messenger boys.

THAT WE MAY BE ONE

Thus the main idea conveyed by the word itself, namely someone who is sent by someone else, is used to describe Christ's ministry (sent by the Father), the Twelve (sent by Christ) other apostles like Paul and Barnabas who worked in a similar way to the Twelve, and messenger boys sent by some of the apostles.

But what is important for us to realize is that nowhere in the New Testament is any provision made for apostolic replacements after the death of the Twelve. If their ministry was as important as the New Testament suggests, and it was God's plan that apostles should continue, then why is there no mention at all of a succession and how it should be maintained?

There are references in the Pastoral Epistles (1 and 11 Timothy, and Titus) to the office and ministry of elders; but no mention of apostles. Some of the apostles were martyred early, yet there is no mention of their sucessors. I believe there can be only one answer: *God never intended there to be any more apostles.*

There is one important incident which sheds light on this whole question: the appointment of Matthias to replace Judas Iscariot after his suicide (see Acts 1:21-26). Some interpret this as a mistaken action, a hasty decision; they believe that the Church ought to have waited a few years and then enrolled Paul as one of the Twelve. That may be true. But let's assume for one moment that the Church did act correctly and was led by the Holy Spirit in what it did. Certainly this must

Apostles and Prophets, True or False?

have been the view of Luke, the author of Acts, or he would not have included the story in his book or, if he had, added some verses by way of reflection on the mistake the Church made, if he had in any way doubted the wisdom of this action.

We need to notice the qualification for being included in the Twelve—"one of the men who have accompanied us during all the time that the Lord Jesus went in and out among us, beginning from the baptism of John until the day when He was taken up from us . . ." (1:21-22). Paul would not have qualified for this. Certainly Paul was an apostle, but he could never have been one of the Twelve, who were a unique group of people united by the fact that Jesus had chosen them to be His assistants during His earthly ministry.

But the main point I want to make is that this procedure is never adopted again. There was something quite unique about this group of people. No one was intended to succeed to their office.

The Role of Apostles

The apostles (the Twelve plus a few others, particularly Paul) had a unique role to play. I deliberately use the word "unique" because, as we shall see, they alone could fulfill the role assigned to them in God's plans and purposes. Their role was two-fold and relates to the Church and the Scriptures.

1) *They were the founders of the Christian Church*

Of course, in one sense, Jesus Christ was the

THAT WE MAY BE ONE

Founder of the Church. It is built on Him, He is its chief corner-stone. But in another sense, the apostles of Christ were its founding fathers, Paul declares this in Ephesians 2:20 when he writes about the Church as "built upon the foundation of the apostles and prophets." One thing about a foundation is that it can only be laid once. The first apostles did something unique and were specially endowed to do it. Of course the Church had yet to spread throughout the whole earth and through many centuries. But the Church was never founded again. Many local churches were started in various parts of the world; but these were always extensions of the same organism and, therefore, built on the same foundation.

2) *They were the communicators of the doctrine of Christ*

In the same epistle, Paul also mentioned this equally important role of the early apostles. Paul refers to the revelation of the truth which God had chosen not to reveal to other generations, "as it has now been revealed to His holy apostles and prophets by the Spirit" (3:5). In Acts 2:42 we are told of the early Christians that "they devoted themselves to the apostles' teaching and fellowship." Jesus Christ commissioned the apostles to be the communicators of the truth in a unique sense. Just as the Church cannot be founded again, neither does Christ intend it to add to the Scriptures. The Church has one foundation and one fount of truth, and

Apostles and Prophets, True or False?

it was to the apostles that Christ entrusted these responsibilities.

Succeeding generations of God's people have their responsibilities, too. But no one has been commissioned to found a new church or to add a fresh doctrine. We have, however, all been called to extend the Church of Jesus Christ throughout the whole world and to build on the apostolic foundations. We have also been commissioned to proclaim the apostolic truth and fashion our lives according to its precepts and our minds according to its doctrines.

Apostles Today?

We have already noticed that the New Testament uses the word "apostles" in several different ways. I believe we can do so also. The church of the first century was a church "on the move." It flowed all over the place, moving into Jewish and pagan society with ever-increasing success. In that sense the Church was *apostolic* and ought still to be today. The apostolic ministry comprised men (and there is some evidence for women as well) who traveled extensively, planting churches, taking messages, encouraging disheartened Christians, correcting error, and promoting unity and cooperation. But as time went on, we find the word increasingly being dropped from the church vocabulary. By the second century there were no more apostles, certainly with anything like the apostolic authority wielded by men like Peter and Paul. Within a short space of time, bishops were firmly established as the leaders of the leaders in the world-wide Church. How this all evolved, and whether bishops were a development from the apostles or from the elders, is controversial. But what is beyond contradiction is the fact that church government and the authority which was exercised by leaders was in the hands of bishops in a comparatively short time and from that day to this few attempts have been made to resurrect the office and ministry of apostles, except in the wider sense of men and women sent to minister to the world-wide Church and extend its border in all nations.

It is, therefore, a mistake to seek to establish apostles in the Church today, as well as being confusing and divisive. It does not take into consideration existing structures. In by-passing them, it is simply another way of establishing yet another denomination and a new network of authority which makes it much harder for Christians to unite and work constructively together.

Abortive Attempts

There have been three major attempts to bring back apostles in the last century and a half. The Catholic Apostolic church was set up in the last century and appointed twelve apostles. They made no provision for new apostles because they believed that Christ was coming back so soon there would be no further need for them.

All of these apostles have died and so virtually has

Apostles and Prophets, True or False?

that church, and Christ has not yet returned. One of their main arguments was that the long delay in the return of Christ was due to the fact that the apostolic office was so quickly withdrawn. Their cry, "Bring back the apostles," carried the conviction that this would fulfill the one missing condition for the return of Christ. They were wrong in this, though there are many splendid things that they did as a church.

When the Pentecostal Movement began at the beginning of this century, it soon divided into various denominations, the divisions often being because of differences of opinion on church order. One group, the Apostolic church, began in Wales and was the only Pentecostal group in Britain to have apostles and prophets. It spread to the Continent and there are some congregations in France and Denmark. But of all the Pentecostal churches, it has been one of the smallest and has had little influence on the movement as a whole.

Some of the house churches have more recently begun to recognize and appoint "apostles" as leaders, usually with an authority which is wider than their own local church. Thus a rigid hierarchy is developing amongst some of these new house churches. A word which is often used is "covering" to describe a new kind of relationship between Christians, in which one submits to another in order to be "covered" by him. This authority is always male, never female. From the personal it has extended to the corporate, so that leaders may have a "covering" authority over several churches; thus a new denominational pattern is developing in which "apostles" have a part to play not unlike that of Anglican bishops or Methodist chairmen, though with much more authority. It remains to be seen whether they will succeed where the Catholic Apostolics failed in the last century. The present signs are not hopeful.

Discernment of Apostles

Obviously there is a need for careful discernment in this matter, a point which the New Testament makes quite forcefully. Both Jesus (Rev. 2:2) and Paul (2 Cor. 11:13) warned churches about "false apostles." In Paul's case he is quite specific as to who they were. It has sometimes been said that the mention of *false* apostles implies that there must at the same time be *true* apostles, and, therefore, the Lord always intended the office of apostle to continue within the Church.

Actually Christ himself in the gospels never mentioned false apostles, although He did warn the Church about false Christs and false prophets. But the above argument falls down when we consider Jesus' warning about false Christs (Mark 13:22). We are hardly to expect true Christs because Jesus mentioned false Christs! There is only one true Christ. But, as we shall now see, there is a proper place for apostolic ministries today, even though apostles as such were only intended for the first-century Church.

Apostles and Prophets, True or False?

Apostolic Ministry Today

If Jesus never intended apostles in His Church after the death of the last of the Twelve (probably John), He certainly intended that His Church should continue to be apostolic both in the power of the Holy Spirit, and in the manner of its life and ministry. There is that other sense in which the word "apostle" is used in the New Testament to describe a variety of ministries. What distinguished these ministries from others was that they were trans-local. They were travelers not settlers. In the local churches from earliest times, it was the elders who exercised authority. Apostles did have a trans-local authority also. But this role was continued, not by new apostles, but by bishops, who were elders with a trans-local ministry, serving not the local church but a number of churches in a geographical area which became known as a diocese.

But there was also a variety of "apostolic" or traveling ministries which worked alongside, though sometimes in competition with, the diocesan structures. We saw this in more detail in chapter 5 when we considered the way two kinds of structure developed within the early church and afterwards. Thus apostolic bands, of which the Twelve were a prototype, continued to serve the universal Church, and to fulfill an apostolic ministry from that day to this. They also, as we have seen, fulfilled the Great Commission to spread the Good News throughout the earth. In a sense, all missionaries are "apostles" or have an apostolic function. So also evangelists like

THAT WE MAY BE ONE

Billy Graham and Luis Palau serve this apostolic function in the area of evangelism.

The Charismatic Movement has spawned many apostolic-type ministries. It coincided with the advent of the jet aero engine and its development in civil aviation which revolutionized world travel and has made world-wide apostolic ministries comparatively easy. Men and women now minister all over the world and have ministries which reach millions through TV, radio and tape recordings. But these people are only "apostles" in a secondary sense, and, if they are wise, they will submit wherever they go to the existing structure of authority which is the on-going framework of the Church all over the world. They are there to serve the Church, not build their own personal empires.

The Church has always been charismatic. But when the fires burn low and the Church cools off, God has always raised up those who challenge it and lead it in new ways. Constantly there has been tension between these two elements. God has chosen to use as His instruments men and women with remarkable spiritual charisma who have been a gift to the whole Church, not to one small part of it. When the light shines and the fires are re-kindled, it would be wrong to keep it all to oneself, even if that were possible. People are drawn to the fire like a magnet. So traveling becomes inevitable. Either people go on their own pilgrimages to centers of renewal and those people associated with them, as with John the Baptist and the Curé d'Ars, or

Apostles and Prophets, True or False?

these "apostolic" figures take to the road (or air these days). They can be a threat to the establishment, but they have often been God's instruments in the renewal of the Church. Here, too, we see the extension of the apostolic ministry.

What About the Prophets?

In the two key passages in Ephesians 2:20 and 3:5, which I have already mentioned, Paul links together apostles and prophets. So we need also to look at the office of "prophet" in this chapter.

The question we need to address is a plain one. If there are no apostles in the New Testament sense today, are there any prophets? I think the answer must be "no" and for the same reasons. The apostolic and prophetic ministries were foundational in a unique sense. Many since have been called upon to lay foundations. There have been missionaries who have founded churches, men and women who have founded religious orders and communities, as well as a multitude of Christian organizations from the Y.M.C.A. to the W.C.C. and from the Salvation Army to the Focalare. In that secondary sense, we might call them "apostles" or "prophets." But all these new Christian adventures, if they are true to the Lord Jesus Christ, are built on the apostolic foundation which is unique and unrepeatable.

Many people also have been inspired to catch fresh glimpses and receive new insights into the word of God and the revelation of Jesus Christ. But no one has

THAT WE MAY BE ONE

been given new revelation. The canon of the Scriptures is closed. The Book of Revelation is the final revelation and anyone who adds to it is in some danger and is certainly self-deceived. The prophets had a unique function in those early days which no one has had since; and so, like the apostles, the prophets dropped quietly from the scene.

There is another reason why I believe we are not today to expect prophets according to this earlier pattern. In the book of the prophet Joel there is a famous prophecy in which the promise is given that there will come a day when God will pour out His Spirit "on all flesh," and "sons and daughters" would prophesy, even "menservants and maidservants." In other words, the prophetic gift would no longer be restricted to a few individual prophets, but all God's people would be prophetic. We still hear about the "priesthood of all believers," but not very often about the "prophethood of all believers." Just as all true believers can now, through the blood of Christ, enter in the Holy of Holies and have fellowship and communion with God, for the veil of the Temple has been torn in half, so also all true believers can "read, mark, learn and inwardly digest" the word of God and then communicate it to others, and thus be "prophets" today.

Having said this, I would hasten to add two important points. I have already shown how, in a secondary sense, there are men and women today who have "apostolic" ministries. I believe the same is

Apostles and Prophets, True or False?

true of the prophetic ministry. All through the centuries, there have been people who have been gifted and inspired to see things clearly and speak the word of God with particular relevance and incisiveness. I don't believe we should call them prophets as such. Most, if not all of them, have had other distinctive ministries which they have combined with this one. In the last century there were secular prophets like Charles Dickens, who used his gifts of writing to warn his readers about the social and economic evils of his day, and H.G. Wells, who was an avowed agnostic and yet who saw "the shape of things to come" with remarkable accuracy. He died in London during the war-time blitz, literally hearing their fulfillment and incapable of finding any answer to what he was experiencing, because he was so out of touch with God.

Writers seem to have a special ministry in this respect. Is it because they have to spend many hours on their own and so have a greater capacity for listening than most people? In this century we have had the prophetic writings of George Orwell, in particular his now-famous prophecies about 1984. But to match that man's secular viewpoint, we have more recently the prophetic writings of Alexander Solzhenitsyn which have been deeply Christian.

The other important point I want to make is that although I don't believe in the office of prophet, I do believe it has been God's will that the gift of prophecy should continue in the Church from the first century

THAT WE MAY BE ONE

until the Lord returns. There is no indication anywhere in the New Testament that the gift of prophecy is to be withdrawn. It has its weaknesses, because it comes through our weak and sinful human natures. Paul tells us in 1 Corinthians 13:9, "our prophecy is imperfect." But it is still God's will for His people and we must not, as Paul elsewhere put it, "despise prophesying" (1 Thess. 5:20). Rather we are to desire earnestly the gifts of the Holy Spirit, especially that of prophecy (1 Cor. 14:1). We should both expect and welcome this gift in the Church, though also being careful to discern whether it is from God or not.

13

The Spotless Church

> *Husbands, love your wives, as Christ loved the Church and gave himself up for her, so that He might sanctify her, having cleansed her by the washing of water with the word, and He might present the Church to himself in* splendor, without spot or wrinkle or any such thing, *that she might be holy and without blemish. Even so husbands should love their wives as their own bodies.* (Eph. 5:25-38)

This passage is being quoted at the present time as a justification for the creation of new churches and for people to leave the historic churches to join these new fellowships. It is usually linked with the expectation that Jesus Christ is returning to this earth quite soon. The argument goes something like this. Jesus Christ is coming soon. He is coming back for His bride, the Church. The bride is being prepared and is to be "without spot or wrinkle." The historic churches are so compromised morally and doctrinally, and are impossible to renew, and the time is so short, we must

THAT WE MAY BE ONE

leave these sinking ships and get into the new church which is now in the final stages of preparation for the marriage feast of the Lamb.

There are two flaws in this argument. The first is the assumption that the return of Christ is imminent. I want to challenge that later in the chapter. The second is the interpretation of this particular passage. We need to turn to that now.

The Perfect Church?

Paul has dealt with the subject of the Church in chapter 4 of Ephesians. Here in chapter 5 he is teaching about practical issues arising from marriage and family relationships and those we have at work. The context is *marriage* not the *Church*. It is true that Paul does relate the marriage contract to that between Christ and the Church. If this passage is a justification for Christians leaving the imperfect churches for the spotless variety, whatever that may be, would it not also be a justification for husbands or wives contracting out of imperfect marriages? The passage, however, is urging husbands to be as faithful and loving to their wives as Christ is to the Church, which He desires to sanctify because it is so obviously in practice unsanctified.

The primary teaching in this passage is about marriage and particularly the husband-wife relationship. Paul illustrates that relationship with the one that exists between Christ and the Church. Husbands are to behave towards their wives as Christ behaves

The Spotless Church

towards the Church. But the key matter is that of timing. Does the presentation of the Church (without spot or wrinkle) take place before or after the return of Christ? Here the subject (marriage) and the illustration (Christ and the Church) are different in their respective time scales. In the husband-wife relationship, the marriage has already taken place. The words "husband," "wife" are meaningful only after marriage. But the marriage of Christ to the Church is yet to happen. In the husband-wife relationship, the sanctification process follows the marriage. In the Christ-Church relationship, it precedes it.

If we take this passage and compare it with others, we have to say that the perfection of the Church, its glorification, its condition of being "without spot or wrinkle," cannot refer to its condition on earth before Christ's return, but must refer to its heavenly or final condition *after* the return. In the New Testament, the tenses of sanctification are not the same in every passage. "Sanctification" is a word used both to describe the *condition* of all Christians, irrespective of their spiritual state, and also the *process* by which they are being made more like Christ. Thus in 1 Corinthians 1:2, Paul refers to the Corinthian Christians of all people as "sanctified in Christ Jesus" and reminds them in 6:11 that they were "sanctified." In the Jewish marriage service, the bridegroom says to the bride at the giving of the ring, "Behold, thou art sanctified to me." So in that sense the Church is already sanctified or "without spot or wrinkle," however imperfect and

THAT WE MAY BE ONE

faithless it may be. The Eastern Orthodox Church has maintained this scriptural emphasis for centuries. For them it is almost blasphemous to talk about "renewing the Church" because it is already perfect in so far as it is the Body of Christ, and it would be blasphemous to think of renewing Christ.

However, the Scriptures do also teach the need for the sanctifying process of God's grace leading us to perfection—a state of blessedness which is only possible in heaven and which will be the happy lot of all God's people when Christ returns.

But in this particular passage, what is Paul saying? It is unnecessary to come down on one side or the other. All we need to show is that the popular view that Christ is preparing a spotless Church on this earth cannot possibly be what Paul had in mind.

If we interpret Paul's words according to the first view, then the Church is already without spot or wrinkle, the historic churches and all the rest. If we take the second view, namely that sanctification is a process, then the state of perfection is unobtainable in this life and on this earth. It must refer to the stage of the Church *after* it has been glorified, that is *after* Christ has returned, when He will finally do away with all sin and make the Church perfect to be His bride forever. In other words, it *cannot* mean that the spotless condition will take place before Christ comes again, unless in the sense that it is already (and always has been) in that condition. In which case, the modern, new and special interpretation which refers it to new

The Spotless Church

churches in contrast to the old and "spotty" variety is fallacious.

The other question we need to ask is, who makes the presentation of the bride? Or in other words, who gives the bride away? Paul is clear: it happens to be the Bridegroom! It is Jesus Christ who presents the Church. It is not for us to present the Church to Christ. He does that himself. He is the only one fit to do it. Christ is not coming back for a perfect Church here on earth; but when He does return He will perfect His Church in preparation for the marriage and eternal bliss in the glory of heaven.

Is Christ Coming Soon?

There are some who believe the answer is "yes." Well-known charismatic leaders have said publicly that they believe He is going to return during their lifetime. For some, this is an added reason for leaving the old churches and preparing new churches for His coming. It is for them justification for doing things which they would not otherwise do.

The problem with countering this sort of argument is that it is unanswerable from the start. One can say, "He is coming soon," but one can never say, "He is not coming soon." In the New Testament, we are warned against setting dates. "It is not for you to know the times or the seasons," Jesus said to the disciples just before Pentecost in answer to their direct question to Him, "Are you *at this time* going to restore the Kingdom of Israel?" We are told to be ready for His

THAT WE MAY BE ONE

coming at any time. It is wrong to speculate on the date of His coming, and equally wrong to say "He is delaying"—or "He is not coming." That is why I have said that the argument is unanswerable. I cannot say, in response to those who are saying, "He is coming soon," "He is not coming soon." I can only say, "none of us knows" and, therefore, those who say His coming is near are mistaken, unless they have received higher reveleation than Christ during His earthly ministry.

Signs of His Coming

There will be some who will respond to this by saying, "But surely Jesus gave us signs which would indicate when His return would take place?" It is true that He did refer to signs, and we will turn our attention to these in a moment; but we must not forget that Jesus' main emphasis in His teaching was that the date was not even known to himself, and, therefore, it was wrong for His disciples to speculate about it. He also made it clear that His Second Coming would be like "a thief in the night" (Matt. 24:42-44 also 1 Thess. 5:2). Thieves do not announce beforehand when they are coming. Nor do we send invitations to thieves. Again, if we are constantly thinking, "We are going to be burgled tonight," we would have a nervous breakdown with harrowing anticipation. But, on the other hand, we don't leave the door open every night and say, "I'm sure we won't be burgled tonight." We take the necessary precautions, knowing that it might happen any night. But we don't let the thing get out of

The Spotless Church

proportion; we carry on with our lives normally. We sleep contentedly, knowing we have taken normal precautions.

So we should seek to live our lives as if Christ is coming back today. But we do our work for the Lord as if He is not coming back for a long time. There was an expectation in Jerusalem during Jesus' life that "the Kingdom of God" was about to appear. The Messianic age was imminent. Of course it was, but not quite the way the Jews expected it. To counter these false expectations, Jesus told a parable about a nobleman who went on a long journey to "receive kingly power" (Luke 19:11 ff.). He called his servants and gave them money, telling them to "trade with these till I come." The Lord is saying the same to His people today: "Get on with the job I have given you and quit speculating about times and seasons. Leave that to me."

But what about the signs Jesus gave His disciples? Actually, Jesus only mentioned two signs of the end of the world which are relevant to this subject. He talked about calamities like wars, famines and earthquakes. He made it clear that these are all part of what is normal in a fallen world. They are not signs of the end. Jesus actually said "the end is not yet" (Mark 13:7). He made statements about Jerusalem and prophesied its fall some forty years later. But that was not to be the end. There are references (such as Luke 21:24) to the restoration of the Jews to Palestine. But again there is no mention of these being a sign of His coming. Only

THAT WE MAY BE ONE

twice does Jesus specifically relate signs to His return and the end of the world.

1) *The evangelization of the world*

In Matthew 24:14 Jesus makes the statement, "and this gospel of the Kingdom will be preached throughout the whole world as a testimony to all nations; *and then the end will come."* Jesus clearly links His coming with the task of world evangelization. During the twentieth century, the Church has expanded rapidly, particularly in South America, Africa and parts of Asia. But so has the population of the world, and the Church's task is still a daunting one. In Africa, about six million people are added every year to the Church, but there are still areas of the continent in which the gospel has never been preached. This is even more true of Asia where the two countries with the largest populations in the world, India and China, are still largely unevangelized. Progress is being made rapidly but we are still not within sight of the goal that Christ has for the evanglization of the world.

2) *Cosmic disorders*

Jesus also spoke about signs in the heavens. Just as His first coming was announced by the star which brought the wise men from the East, so His Second Coming will be preceded by a veritable cosmic fireworks display. He spoke of, "signs in sun and moon and stars, and upon the earth distress of nations in perplexity at the roaring of the sea and the waves, men

The Spotless Church

fainting with fear and with foreboding of what is coming on the world; for the powers of the heavens will be shaken" (Luke 21:25-26). It is *then* that Jesus says He will come and we are to raise our heads "because your redemption is drawing near." It seems there will be a shaking of the very foundations of the universe which will terrify people. It will be the cue for God's people, however, to look up and know that Christ will soon be arriving. It would seem that these signs will come immediately, perhaps a matter of hours before Christ returns. Quite obviously these signs are not yet in evidence; when they are, they will be beyond doubt and self-authenticating. The whole world will be vividly and dramatically aware of them.

I think it may be right to add a third sign: the unity of God's people. In John 17, Jesus prayed fervently that His people might be one. It is hardly likely that Jesus will come again with the prayer unanswered. Although much progress has been made during this century with the cause of Christian unity, there is still a long way to go. *Those who are fragmenting the Church still further, by setting up new independent Churches, may in fact be hindering rather than hastening Christ's return.* But we must be fair. Those who are not faithful to Christ in the Churches are also to blame. They have often been responsible for creating the situations which have encouraged the development of new churches. Jesus is coming back for a united people, and insofar as we are seeking in prayer and action for the visible unity of God's people, we are hastening the coming of Christ.

Obedience Not Signs

We are not then to say, "He is coming soon" or "He is not coming soon." We are to leave all that to the Father. Nor are we to do anything or refrain from doing anything because we think He is coming soon. There is no justification for us leaving our Churches and joining others in order to prepare ourselves for His coming. If we move at all, it should be solely because the Lord tells us to. The time of His coming, in this respect, is irrelevant. As Martin Luther put it, "even if the world comes to an end tomorrow we will still, in spite of that, plant our little apple tree today." Let me repeat: we are to live as if Christ is coming back tomorrow. But we do the work of the Kingdom as if He is not coming back for a thousand years.

So far as the cosmic disorders are concerned, the signs in the skies, we must leave that to the Lord. They will be clear enough when it is time for them to appear. The whole world will see them and will be thrown into a panic. But the other signs of His coming should radically affect our lives. By putting our backs into the task of world evangelization, and by seeking the reconciliation of Christians and their visible unity, we are hastening the Second Coming of Christ. *God's concern over the timing is the salvation of the world, not the fulfillment of proof texts.* If He is slow, then it is because He does not wish "that any should perish, but

The Spotless Church

that all should reach repentance" (2 Pet. 3:9). Although the Church will not be ageless and spotless when the Lord returns, we believe that in that moment of glorification it will receive its final and complete cleansing to make it ready for the marriage with Christ, the Bridegroom. Only then will the Church be perfect as God is perfect.

14
I'm Staying in!

Many Christians have had or will have to face the problems which I have outlined in this book. Some, like myself, have opted to stay in the boat (which some say is sinking fast); others have decided to leave the sinking ship and take to the small lifeboats which surround the old hulk. Alas, some of these have sprung a leak and have sunk more quickly than the old ship they have left. Others have been skippered by enthusiastic but amateurish seamen who know little about the vagaries of the sea, and have found themselves tossed to and fro on the high seas. They have not a few times cast an envious glance at the grand old ship. It is still afloat and somewhat more stable and built to last and to survive the worst gales.

Actually, the great ship is *not* sinking. It is certainly heavily loaded. There have been not a few mutinies and it has lost a sense of direction. It is not quite sure where it is going. But it is going to be around for a long time to come. It is good to see some of the small lifeboats coming back to the ship having realized that their abandoning it was after all a little premature, and important changes are taking place on board which

THAT WE MAY BE ONE

are encouragements to the faithful, if at times disheartened, members of the crew.

One of the most famous radicals, who has been forced to face this issue, is Hans Kung. In his book, *On Being a Christian,* he describes those who have, unlike himself, opted to leave the Roman Catholic church.

> They jumped ship as an act of honesty, of courage, of protest, or even simply as a last resort, because they could endure no more. But for us would it not be finally an act of despair, an admission of failure, a capitulation? We were with it in better times: are we now to abandon the boat in the storm and leave others, with whom we used to sail, to steer against the wind, bale out the water and perhaps to fight for survival? We have received so much in this community of faith that we cannot so easily get out of it. We have become so involved in change and renewal that we cannot disappoint those who have shared our commitment. We should not provide this joy for the opponents of renewal nor inflict this sorrow on our friends . . .

The alternative has yet to convince me. To break away from the rest of the Church seems inevitably to lead to an unhealthy isolation and quite quickly to new institutions. It is amazing how soon radicals become

I'm Staying in!

conservatives fighting to preserve their "new thing." Elitist Christianity has always proved an illusion and church utopias have always ended in disappointment. Actually the weaker the Church becomes, the more lovable it seems. Can we not join with Hans Kung and say, "We love this Church as it is now and as it could be . . . I am not staying in the Church *although* I am a Christian. It is *because* I am a Christian that I am staying in the Church"?

The Moslems have a simple way of describing "independency": "mosques of one and a half bricks." One cannot see the future of the Church in terms of the multiplication of churches of one and a half bricks. The present situation of the world church would indicate that the house church approach can only operate as a tiny segment of it. It is significant. It is real. But it is totally unrealistic to imagine that it can ever form more than a small part of the universal Church that Christ loved and died for. So it is essential that alongside the independent line that some are taking, the rest of us continue to work together for renewal and reconciliation. What place, for example, has this new approach in Scandinavia where the Lutheran church forms the overwhelming majority of the Christian presence? If Scandinavia is going to be significantly reached with the gospel, it has to come largely through the Lutheran church, which, incidentally, has successfully given hospitality to numerous renewal movements in the past. The same can be said of Poland, where the Christian presence is Roman

THAT WE MAY BE ONE

Catholic, Russia where it is Eastern Orthodox, Egypt where it is Coptic, and Fiji where it is Methodist, to give a few examples.

Those who sail small boats will know that when you capsize there are two golden rules. Don't panic, and stay with the boat. The temptation to leave the boat and strike out for the shore is overwhelming at times, but it needs to be firmly resisted. The boat is more likely to remain afloat than the sailor! So we also need to resist similar temptations in the choppy seas of our day, when the wind howls through the rigging and the boat so easily capsizes. Don't panic, even when you see others deserting their boats. Stay with the boat.

The Cost

There is a cost to pay for the unity that God wants for His people. It is not easy to evaluate who suffers more, those who stay in the historic churches and face the music, or those who leave. It is a costly thing to see things which others don't see, and to stay in a situation in which you will be misunderstood and abused, sometimes by those closest to you. One man who faced up to all this and suffered the consequences is David du Plessis, known affectionately as "Mr. Pentecost." When I first got to know him, he constantly urged me to stay in the Anglican church and remain faithful both to it and to the witness I was called to give to spiritual renewal within it. He was asking me to do something which he had done for many years himself. He grew up in a Pentecostal home

I'm Staying in!

in South Africa. His parents were Pentecostals. David remains to this day a faithful Pentecostal. When he began to witness personally to the World Council of Churches and later became an unofficial observer at Vatican II, his status as a Pentecostal came under sharp attack. The Assemblies of God in America withdrew his papers. But David did not withdraw. Each year he faithfully attended their conferences. He never spoke out against them. He remained a faithful Pentecostal son. It is good to know that he is again recognized by the Assemblies of God, but for many years David's ministry and witness was extremely costly.

During 1980, David visited the church I was a member of in London and spoke at an evening meeting. After he had finished speaking, I was given a prophecy. It happened to be tape recorded so I took it with me to Canada a few weeks later and shared it at a conference in Toronto. One of the conference delegates was Mrs. Ruth Fazal, a member of an Anglican church in that city and a fine singer. When she heard the prophecy she set the words to music and sang them on the "100 Huntley Street" television program. She has now produced an album with the title of that song. It is called, "Crown of Glory, Crown of Thorns." It describes the costliness of Christian unity, the pathway David du Plessis and many others have trodden. I would like to end this book with it.

THAT WE MAY BE ONE

O children I am wanting you to see
The cost of my call to unity;
It is not an easy road to go along,
For the shadow of My cross lies on that way . . .

Refrain:
I'm not putting on your head a crown of glory,
But I'm putting on your head a crown of thorns,
I'm not taking you along an easy road,
But a stony way is My way, won't you come?

I am calling you to humble yourselves,
Not only to Me, but to each other;
Refrain from the accusing of one another,
For My people, this is grieving unto Me . . .

I am calling you to be in this world,
A light and a leaven to all people;
But I'm grieved at how you cut each other down,
And I'm grieved at the hardness of your hearts . . .

All your praises are not pleasing to Me,
For your hearts are disobedient and stubborn;
All the offerings that you give Me, they mean nothing,
For you will not let your lives be ruled by Me . . .

O My children, look to Jesus, your Saviour,
So humble and loving and forgiving,
Are you ready now to go this way I'm calling,
And be obedient unto Me, so I can bless you? . . .

Acknowledgements

I want to acknowledge my debt to those whose contributions have significantly influenced this book. There are two in particular, Ralph D. Winter for his essay "The Two Structures of God's Redemptive Mission" published in *Missiology: An International Review,* which influenced chapter 5, and Michael Griffiths for a talk given in September, 1982 which influenced chapter 6. Ralph Winter's essay can be obtained from the William Carey Library Publishers, P.O. Box 128-C, Pasadena, California 91104, U.S.A.

I also want to thank Mrs. Ruth Fazal for her permission to print the words of her song "Crown of Glory, Crown of Thorns" in chapter 14.

All biblical references are from the Revised Standard Version unless otherwise indicated.

Michael Harper
January 1983